Tech Tactics
Money Saving Secrets

by William Keeley

Tech Tactics – Money Saving Secrets
First Edition

ISBN-10: 1460984390
ISBN-13: 978-1460984390

Kindle Edition ASIN:B004WKT03C
Nook Edition BNID: 2940012361844

Table of Contents

Chapter 4 - Entertainment and Education 101

Introduction

The intent of this book is to allow the reader to save money by using free or very inexpensive devices, programs, and services in order to save money while enjoying modern technology. People pay too much money for things that can be had very cheaply or for free if one only knew where to find the goodies. This book is about how to take advantage of technology without having to pay huge sums of money to big business. The author concentrates on tips, tactics, devices, programs, and secrets that actually work (at least at the time this book is written). It is the hope that when a reader reads and uses just one thing learned in this book that the book will pay for itself. This books offers something for everyone from a relative beginner to the hardcore geek. Even though there are free and inexpensive products available that do the same thing as their higher priced commercial counterparts, the products are usually not clones of the of the more expensive products. What this means is that their user interface or the way users interact with these programs may be somewhat different. In other words, if one is already used to using the more expensive products, he or she will have to get used to how the less expensive counterpart works. In most cases, people can get used to the free or inexpensive products rather quickly.

Many free and inexpensive products and services related to technology exist for various reasons. Some of these reasons include producers wanting to make something that everyone can use for free in order to make a name for themselves, producers who want to use a free product to entice potential buyers into looking at products for sale, producers who made a product for themselves who have decided to contribute same in the hope that others find it useful as well, hobbyists who just enjoy creating, and those who want to to use their products to to install ad-ware, spy-ware, or other nefarious technology.

This book discuss the advantages and pitfalls in using free and inexpensive inexpensive technology products. Most products discussed in this book come with no strings attached. The products that do have strings attached are pointed out, and exactly what strings are explained. There are many free products available. Microsoft office can cost anywhere between one hundred and several hundred dollars.

There is a free program that will do almost everything Microsoft Office will that is legally available on-line for absolutely no cost to the user. The best part is the fact that this program contains no ad-ware or spy-ware. It comes with no strings attached. Even though long distance telephone service is getting less expensive each year, it is still pricey compared to the free and less expensive options that are currently available for those "in the know." Many people pay tens and in some cases over one hundred dollars a month so that they can watch decent television programming. In addition to paying these high rates, they often have to put up with annoying advertisements disrupting their viewing pleasure. There are free alternatives with fewer commercials or none at all.

Other people, when their computer

slows to a crawl, will take their computer to a repair shop and pay tens to hundreds of dollars getting it back up to speed. Those "in the know" do it quickly and easily themselves using programs already installed on the computer or freely available on-line.

Some people spend tens of dollars per computer per year to protect their computer against malicious software. Others use products that work as well if not better, and they do so at no cost.

These are just a few of many examples of money savers that can be found in this book. Many computer users spend hours of frustrating searches on the Internet looking for diagnostic and optimization tools to speed up their computers or to make the more reliable. Others are simply looking for software that will make a device such as a printer, web-cam, or tablet device work with their computers. In many cases, they will come across websites featuring products that aim to do what they want. However, once they go through the trouble of downloading, installing, and using the software, the software performs the job as advertised - at least up to a point. The software will tell them what is wrong, and will have a "fix it" or "optimize" button. When the user clicks the button, he or she will see a notice that the software must "be registered" before the action is performed.

Registration usually involves the payment of money or the providing of personal information. The user will usually remove the software or in rarer cases, will pay the money or provide the personal information. The author has had this experience, and has spent hours trying to find the free stuff that actually does the entire job as advertised. Using this book will save the reader many hours of searching, downloading, and installing programs only to find a demand of payment. The author has done the research and legwork to find the gems that will help the reader.

While the intent of the author of this book is to provide the reader with useful information, the author does not have any control over products he has not created. Nor does the author have any control over how the reader uses the products discussed in this book nor the circumstances under which discussed products are used.

Therefore, any use or misuse of information contained in this book is the sole responsibility or the reader.

About the Author

The author of this book, William Keeley, has the gift of high functioning autism and has been involved with computers and electronics for most of his life. While growing up, most of his peers were out playing sports or were involved in highly social activities while William was studying, researching, learning, programming, and making things. As a result of this, William has built up vast stores of knowledge and experience and wants to offer readers the benefits of thirty one years of study, experience, and hard work in computer related disciplines. In high school during the mid 1980's, William has won multiple awards at academic contests related to mathematics and computer science. Some of these include third place in Geometry at Chipola College Math Olympiad, first place in Computer Literacy at George C. Wallace College two years in a row, and third place in Computer Programming at George C. Wallace. He also won first place in Data Processing Concepts two years in a row in district Future Business Leaders Association of America. William has also helped both students and teachers with computer related questions and problems throughout his high school career and continues to do so to this day.

William Keeley is also listed in Who's Who among America's Junior Colleges and was on the dean's list during his career at Chipola College. He is also a graduate of the U.S. Navy's Nuclear Field "A" School in Electronics.

William has worked in several different occupations relating to computers, telephones, and electronics. This includes employment as a telephone technician, computer technical support agent, assistant systems administrator for a Fortune 500 company, a sales maker for a large electronics chain, and a computer integration technician (lots of programming) for a small electronics company. All of these jobs has allowed William to gain his real world, common sense experience relating to technology.

William has installed and used several operating systems on his personal computers. These include CP/M, MS-DOS, Windows 3.11, SCO Unix, Debian Linux, Slackware Linux, Windows 95, Windows 98, Windows XP, his own custom made distribution of Linux, Gentoo Linux, Mandriva Linux, and Windows 7.

William has used and worked on computers running Solaris and BSD Unix as well.

William is also a self taught programmer who has studied and used BASIC, Assembly Language, C, C++, and Java. In finding study materials, William has had to wade through tons of junk information in order to get to the real gems that are available on-line. William has also designed, set up and installed his own phone and security system.

William currently is a self employed computer consultant and an I.T. Instructor who teaches students with Asperger's Syndrome. William's goal is to teach real world problem solving based on technical knowledge and common sense.

Acknowledgments

Thanks to all of the people in my life that have made this book possible. Without their input and inspiration, and plain goading, I would have never written this book.

I would like to thank my mom, Dolores Rountree, my stepdad, Kent Rountree, for reading this book and helping me decide how to make things clearer to the average computer user.

I would also like to thank Anthony Gaudiano of the Congregation of Yahweh in Panama City, Florida for suggesting that I write this book, goading me into doing it, and his help in editing the contents. Anthony and other members of the congregation have lent their support to me over the last ten years in this endeavor as well as many others.

Another person, Cody Deese who is a student of mine, has provided me with technical insights and suggestions that I might have overlooked. His technical prowess is something I admire and find rare in today's youth.

I would also like to thank Helen Ezell and all the rest of the staff of the Autism Education Center in Lynn Haven, Florida for the use of their facilities and giving me a voice in teaching and demonstrating many of the tech tactics listed in this book.

Most of all, I would like to thank Yahweh, Creator of the universe as well as His Son, Yahshua, for blessing me with the people, knowledge, mind, and talent that has made it possible for me to write this book.

Chapter 1 Computer Repair

Whether one is considering doing his or her own computer repair to save money, learn more about computers, or even to open a service or business, he or she can have a set up to do so with a very minimum investment. For the do it yourself-er, that cost may be as low as the price of a couple of blank CD'S. For a well equipped small repair service, the price may climb to a few hundred dollars. This chapter gives information on basic facilities, tools, equipment, software, and techniques for a wide range of computer repairs from installing operating systems and motherboards to simply giving a computer a quick tune up.

Facilities, Tools, and Equipment

Someone who is simply repairing his or her computer may be able to use their kitchen or coffee table or even their computer desk for the job. For many problems, it may not even be necessary to remove the cover from the computer. In fact, most computer problems are software related. A sluggish computer can in many cases be brought back up to speed by doing a few simple things. For people who have a decent amount of skill and knowledge, they can make extra money or even repair computers for their main livelihood.

People can set up an efficient and lucrative shop for under $200. The good thing is the fact that most of the things listed here can be obtained either for free or for an ultra low price. A computer shop consists of a place to work as well as a minimum of tools, hardware, and software to efficiently accomplish a repair task. The things listed here will allow a technician to fix over 98% of computers that arrive in the shop. One may even have most of the things listed already at hand.

A minimum amount of hardware is needed to troubleshoot incoming computers. Items needed include a screw driver kit, ground strap, power supply, monitor, keyboard, mouse, backup media, multimeter, vacuum, and/or compressed air. The screw driver kit is one of the most necessary and cheapest items that is absolutely necessary for computer hardware repair. It is used to assemble and disassemble computers in the event of hardware related issues. Another item that is not absolutely necessary but which can make life easier is a ground strap. This item consists of an arm band that is connected to a ground in order to prevent damaging static buildup. Static discharge can also be provided by other means as well. These include not wearing shoes (alone in a shop), touching the chassis of computers while extracting parts, and touching a person's skin before handing a part to him or her. A known good power supply is required in order to properly troubleshoot computers that have startup issues. The power supply does not actually have to be installed in the computer itself, but it does have to provide the proper electrical power. A power supply should have long enough cables to connect to all of the hard disks, CD/DVD drives as well as the hard drives. A known good monitor is also necessary to troubleshoot a computer. One of the most important pieces of equipment to have is a mass storage media that can store the files of any computer that is being repaired. This needs to be used in order to protect the software and data on on one's computer in case of a crash or other catastrophic event.

Standard Computer Service

Standard service steps should be taken on any Microsoft Windows computer one is repairing unless there is some specific reason not to do so. These steps generally speed up the computer and remove software that slow down the computer or cause problems. They also repair many errors on disks and may prevent greater problems. It is generally recommended to perform the steps in the order they are listed, but if there are problems performing some of the steps, they may be postponed until other procedures are done. In fact, it is recommended that these steps be done at least one or two times a month. It is always a very good idea to backup all important files on your computer in case of the rare event of a problem. It is a good idea to have the original operating system's disk in case something goes terribly wrong. However, as a general rule, these tasks cause no problems and greatly increase the performance of a computer.

Backup and Imaging

When repairing a computer that has software or file-system issues, it is always a good idea to make either a mirror image, a file by file backup, or even both. Doing this will save tremendous heartache in the case something goes wrong. One free software package that will allow one to clone a hard drive is a bootable CD called, "Clonezilla." Clonezilla is available for free download at http://clonezilla.org. This package will allow one to backup a hard-drive and restore it exactly as backed up. It will also allow one to replace a hard drive with another one of equal or greater capacity and allow the computer to retain all of its settings, installed software, data files and everything else and the computer it is used on should behave exactly the same as it did before a hard drive swap. In fact, the computer may exhibit even better performance than it did before. Another option is to create a subdirectory on a mass storage device such as a terabyte hard drive and then just drag and drop files from the drive to be backed up into the subdirectory. The author usually does both.

File-system check

CHKDSK is a program that comes with most Windows based computers. It serves to run diagnostic tests on the file-system and hard drive itself. It can be set to repair most disk file-system errors. File system errors can usually be repaired using this method. Errors on the file-system can lead to poor performance, data corruption, and even a nonfunctional operating system.

On Windows XP, Vista, and similar, it is usually run by clicking Start, Run, and typing in chkdsk /f and pressing enter. A message will appear stating, "Chkdsk cannot be run because the volume is in use by another process. Would you like to schedule this volume to be checked the next time the system restarts? (Y/N)?" Simply hit 'y' and press enter.

Restart the computer and allow the

chkdsk program to run. One may want to run the chkdsk program on all the partitions that Windows normally opens This can be done by using the command chkdsk /f D: etc. Now that errors on the windows file system are (hopefully) corrected, the other steps should be less complicated.

On Windows 7, checking the file-system can be accomplished in a slightly different way. Click on the start button, then choose computer. There should be a header that says, "Hard Disk Drives." If there are no hard disk (C: for example) listed, then double click on the "Hard disk drives" header so that the hard disk shows up. After that step, right click with the right mouse button on the disk to be checked (C: for example) and then left click on properties. On the window that opens next, click on the "Tools" tab. Next, click on the "Check now..." button. On the window that opens, put a check-mark in the box next to, "Automatically fix file-system errors" and then click the "Start" button in that same window. One last message will appear. It will say, "Windows can't check the disk while it is in use." Simply click the "Schedule disk check" button and restart the computer.

Defragmenting

Hard disk defragmenting can be one of the most time consuming processes when it comes to speeding up a computer. This is especially true if this task has not been done for a long time. Disk fragmentation occurs when files are written, deleted, changed, etc. What happens is that different portions of a file may be stored on different areas of the hard drive. When file fragmentation occurs, the hard disk drive has to move its read write heads to each part of the hard drive platter where data is stored. In other words, if a file is stored at 5 different areas on the hard drive, the hard drive has to make at least 5 different mechanical movements just to load this one file. This takes time and also produces wear and tear on the hard drive itself. De-fragmenting allows all the file portions to be stored near each other on the hard-drive platter therefore requiring less mechanical movement in order to read the file.

Hard disk defragmenting is usually very easy to accomplish   It is recommended that a file-system check be done before defragmenting is attempted.

On Windows XP and Vista, One can

defragment a hard drive by clicking on Start, All Programs, Accessories, System Tools, and then Disk Defragmenter. Click Drive C and then Defragment. Do this with each volume listed.

On Windows 7, de-fragmenting the disk can be accomplished in a slightly different way. Click on the start button, then choose computer. There should be a header that says, "Hard Disk Drives." If there are no hard disk (C: for example) listed, then double click on the "Hard disk drives" header so that the hard disk shows up. After that step, right click with the right mouse button on the disk to be defragmented (C: for example) and then left click on properties. On the window that pops open, choose tools. Then, click on the "Defragment Now..." button. After that is done, highlight the drive to be defragmented and then click on the "Defragment" button. Each hard drive listed should be defragmented.

Mal-ware Removal

Malicious software includes ad-ware, spy-ware, root-kits, bots, and a whole host of baddies on a computer. There are several products that can clean a computer up for free. These include on-line virus scans such as http://housecall.trendmicro.com, http://www.bitdefender.com/scanner/online/free.html, http://www.pandasecurity.com/homeusers/solutions/activescan/, as well as many others. Unfortunately, many of the on-line mal-ware scanning tools require Internet Explorer in order to work. Another great free ware program that does a very good job of detecting and removing malicious software is Mal-

ware Bytes Antimalware. It is available at
http://www.malwarebytes.org.

The author uses Antimalware to clean most of his clients' infected computers. If an infection is suspected, and nothing seems to clean it up, then the author recommends an anti-malware bootable Linux CD to be used to clean up the computer. The reason for this is the fact that some malicious software embed themselves so deeply into the operating system files that they are able to trick the anti-virus software and prevent their detection and or removal. There are several free anti malware bootable CD's available on-line. These include

http://www.freedrweb.com/livecd,

http://trinityhome.org/Home/index.php?wpid=1&front_id=12,

http://devbuilds.kaspersky-labs.com/devbuilds/RescueDisk/,

http://download.bitdefender.com/rescue_cd/, as well as many others. If the computer has anti malware software already installed, it should be checked to make sure that it is up to date and has the latest anti malware definitions downloaded. An out of date anti malware software package does very little good and can be worse than not having any protection. This is because what may be installed uses up system resources without providing protection and providing an illusion of protection that is not there. If out of date anti malware software is found, inform the owner of the computer that the software is out of date and why it is not good. Suggest that the owner update the software (if payment is required) or start using free ware programs such as Avast, AVG, Microsoft Security Essentials, ClamAV, etc. Avast and AVG can be used for noncommercial home use.

ClamAV can be used for any purpose. Avast can be found at http://www.avast.com/eng/download-avast-home.html. AVG can be found at http://free.avg.com/us-en/download-avg-anti-virus-free-edition.

Microsoft Security Essentials can be found at http://www.microsoft.com/security_essentials/.

ClamAV can be found at http://www.clamwin.com. ClamAV generally does not provide real time protection out of the box, but real time protection can be set up with free browser and email client extensions. The Firefox web browser can use the Fireclam extension which is available at https://addons.mozilla.org/en-US/firefox/addon/10882 in order to scan downloaded files. The Thunderbird email client can use the clamdrib extension to provide real time incoming email protection. This extension is available at https://addons.mozilla.org/en-US/thunderbird/addon/6663

ClamAV also works with Microsoft Outlook (but not Outlook Express). One of the best feature of Clam Antivirus is the fact that is it free for both home and commercial use. In fact, many corporate Internet appliances that are used to protect business networks use Clam Antivirus as their defense against malicious software.

Clearing Excess Files and Data

If Internet browsing is slow despite having a fast connection, this could be due to the browser checking it's cache file to see if it has pages stored on the hard drive before trying to retrieve them on-line. If the cache folder is filled with lots of files, it can take the web browser a long time to sift through the files to see if any of them relate to the page being downloaded. Since Internet Explorer is such an integral part of Windows, this can slow down other aspects of using Windows as well. In addition, lots of files in cache folders can slow down the process of defragmenting the hard drive and anti malware scanning. The instructions for doing this vary for each version of software, but the following instructions should work with most versions.

To clear cache in Internet Explorer, Click Start, choose Control Panel, click on the Internet Options icon, click the "Delete Files" button then click the "OK" button. When the hourglass icon disappears, click the "OK" button and close out of the Control Panel. To clear cache in the Firefox browser, open the Firefox browser and Click Tools, Options, the "Privacy" tab,, and then the "Clear Now" button. Uncheck everything but cache unless you have a specific reason to clear any of the other stuff. Now, click the "Clear Private Date Now" button. After it is finished working, click the "OK" button and close out of Firefox. This should be done for each user account on the computer by logging in and repeating these steps.

Clean Registry

One of the best things that can be done to help speed up a computer is to clean the registry of bad entries. These bad entries can cause a computer to look for things that are not present or cause the computer to spend time doing things that are not necessary. A free registry cleaning program that that works well is "My Little Registry Cleaner." It is available at http://sourceforge.net/projects/littlecleaner/.

Before making any changes to the Windows registry, it is important to back up the current registry. This can be done by clicking Start, run, and typing in regedit. Once that is opened make sure that all of the categories on the left side are collapsed. Then click on File, and choose export. One should store the backup file in the root directory and not in the My Documents folder. Otherwise a user might see it and click on it to see what it is. Doing that will re-install all of the garbage that was there before cleaning. The author tends to use backup-dd/mm/yy in the filename so that I know when the backup was done. Installing and running the registry cleaner is a good way to speed things up a bit. Another very good and also free of charge program is called Ccleaner. This program not only allows one to scan and clean up the registry as well as cache directories, it also allows one to cleanly un-install many programs. It is available   at http://www.ccleaner.com/downloa d.

Once Ccleaner is installed, it is pretty easy to use. To clean the system, open Ccleaner, and if Windows ask,

"Do you want to allow the following program to make changes to this computer," click yes. Once Ccleaner is up, click on the clean icon (looks like a brush), and then on the Analyze button near the bottom. Once the program finishes the analysis, Click the Run Cleaner button near the bottom. A window will pop up asking, "The process will permanently delete files from your system. Are you sure you want to continue?" Click OK.

After cleaning process is complete, click on the registry icon (looks like stacked blocks). After that, click on the "Scan for Issues" button near the bottom. After process is complete, click the "Fix selected issue..." button near the bottom. Another window will pop up asking, "Do you want to back up changes to the registry?" It is a good idea to do so especially if this is the first time running the program. If the option to back up the registry is chosen, the location where the backup is stored can be chosen by the user. It is a good idea for this location to be written down before the Save button is clicked. The next window that pops up will give the option of fixing issues. Click the "Fix Issue" or "Fix All Selected Issues" button. If the "Fix Issue" button is clicked, the user will have to click this button for each issue to be fixed. After registry issues are fixed, the Ccleaner program can be closed.

The File System check, excess file cleaning, registry cleaning, file defragmenting, and malware removal will usually speed up a computer greatly or keep it running fast. The free programs will usually get the job done. It is usually really easy for a user to do these steps him or her self.

Password Reset and Recovery

For many reasons, people may lose or forget their operating system password. In some cases, they may have purchased a computer from a yard sale or surplus auction only to find that the Windows password has not been provided. There are several ways one can try to either reset or recover this password. The easiest way is to use a CD that is designed for this very purpose. Password recovery and reset software listed comes on bootable CD's. In order to use these, the computer on which they are to be used must be configured to boot from the CD drive first. This can be accomplished by setting the option in BIOS configuration. A software package called, "Offline NT Password & Registry Editor" is available for download at http://pogostick.net/~pnh/ntpass wd/bootdisk.html One can also use the Trinity Rescue anti malware CD referred to in the part about malware removal to accomplish the same thing. Using Trinity Rescue may involve the step of mounting the Windows partition and then typing in winpass, so if one is not very familiar with Linux, the former choice is the best one. A good password recovery tool is Ophcrack. This tool is available at http://ophcrack.sourceforge.net/ and it will recover most passwords in minutes. It is better to try to recover the password rather than erasing it due to the fact that on some computers, the user may have encrypted files. These encrypted files become unavailable should the password be unavailable.

Another type of password recovery or

reset involves the CMOS password. The CMOS password is needed to even start up the computer, and when it is set, the computer will ask for it before the operating splash screen comes up. How one resets the password depends upon the type and model of computer used. This is due to the that fact that the password is set in the hardware or motherboard of the computer itself. The technique for resetting this password can be as simple as removing all power as well the "watch" battery from the motherboard for about a minute to having to bridge pins of a chip on the computer's motherboard and powering on the system. There are some programs available on-line that will allow a user to recover passwords from locked computers simply by deriving the password from a displayed hash when the computer boots up. To use these programs, one must have a second computer on which to run them. The password recovery scripts can be found for free at http://dogber1.blogspot.com/2009/05/table-of-reverse-engineered-bios.html

Many commercial sites have taken this guy's work and use it to charge money for what is essentially free. If this is used to recover just one password in order to allow the use of a computer, then this book has already paid for itself.

It is said that an ounce of prevention is worth a pound of cure. This is especially true when it comes to the recovery of CMOS passwords. Most computer manufacturers set a master CMOS password for each computer they manufacture. In most cases, this information is made available to the owner of a computer provided that he or she can prove ownership of the computer. If the computer is still under warranty, this information can be usually obtained free of charge. Since this is the case, computer owners should call the manufacturer's support number to obtain this information. The owner then should write down this information and keep it in a safe place in case the information is needed in the future after the warranty expires.

Software tools to repair common Windows problems

There are many software related problems that can cause hours of frustration for users. In many cases, if a user tries to repair the problem, it involves many hours of frustration in searching for the solution for the problem on-line as well as the time involved in following the steps provided in various solutions. This part of the this book lists common problems and their solutions. In most cases, the problem can be quickly resolved by using freely downloadable programs. Many antivirus programs embed themselves deeply into the operating system in order to stop malicious software before it has enough time to do damage. Unfortunately, when an antivirus programs malfunction, they can disrupt or slow down computer operation. In many cases, uninstalling the antivirus software takes care of the problem. The same antivirus software can be re-installed or a different antivirus program can be used. Antivirus programs' removal programs are listed on the next pages (links worked at the time this book was written):

Avast

http://files.avast.com/files/eng/aswclear.exe

AVG (The long _____ is actually five underscore characters)

http://www.avg.com/filedir/util/avg_arm_sup_____.dir/avgremover.exe is for 32 bit Windows operating systems.

http://www.avg.com/filedir/util/avg_arv_sup_____.dir/avgremoverx64.exe is for 64 bit Windows operating systems.

Avira

http://dl.antivir.de/down/windows/registrycleaner_en.zip

Bit Defender

http://www.bitdefender.com/files/ KnowledgeBase/file/BitDefender_ Uninstall_Tool.exe is for 32 bit Windows operating systems.

http://www.bitdefender.com/files/ KnowledgeBase/file/BitDefender_ Uninstall_Tool_X64new.exe is for 64 bit Windows operating systems.

Computer Associates

http://homeofficekb.ca.com/CIDoc ument.asp? KDId=3125&Preview=0&Return= 0&GUID=DF325E0AA0AB4264AF4 7E4BEA49F571B Versions 2007/2008

http://homeofficekb.ca.com/CIDoc ument.asp? KDId=3226&Preview=0&Return= 0&GUID=96BF3B21F46C426F89D 3ED40BDD236C3 Version 2009

ESET NOD32

http://www.nod32.nl/download/tool/nod32removal.exe

Kapersky

http://www.kaspersky.com/downloads/products2009/kavremover9.zip

McAfee

http://download.mcafee.com/products/licensed/cust_support_patches/MCPR.exe

Norton

ftp://ftp.symantec.com/public/english_us_canada/removal_tools/Norton_Removal_Tool.exe

Panda

http://support.us.pandasecurity.com/retail/tools/uninst06.exe
Version 2006

http://www.pandasecurity.com/resources/sop/UNINSTALLER_07.exe
Version 2007

http://www.pandasecurity.com/resources/sop/UNINSTALLER_08.exe
Version 2008

http://www.pandasecurity.com/resources/sop/UNINSTALLER_10.exe
Version 2009 and Version 2010

Trend Micro

http://solutionfile.trendmicro.com/solutionfile/TIS/TISTOOL/SupportTool_32-bit.exe For 32 bit operating systems

http://solutionfile.trendmicro.com
/solutionfile/TIS/TISTOOL/Support
Tool_64-bit.exe For 64 bit operating
systems

Windows Live One Care

http://download.microsoft.com/do
wnload/4/c/b/4cb845e7-1076-
437b-852a-
7842a8ab13c8/OneCareCleanUp.e
xe

General software removal programs
not specific to antivirus software can
and often do remove unwanted
programs.

Many of these removal programs
even do a better job of getting rid of
unwanted software that the uninstall
programs provided by the author of
the unwanted program. The uninstall
programs discussed in here are

available as free downloads. Appremover removes most of the popular computer security programs. It is available at http://www.appremover.com/appremover/AppRemover.exe. A list of programs that Appremover removes can be found at http://www.appremover.com/supported-applications.

ZoneAlarm is a firewall program. A firewall filters Internet connections and prevents unauthorized programs from being able to access the Internet. Most of the time, ZoneAlarm works great, but in the case where it malfunctions, it can slow or completely block Internet access for some or all programs, When ZoneAlarm malfunctions, it can be removed with this free program available from

http://download.zonealarm.com/b
in/free/support/cpes_clean.exe.

Flash is used on many different websites. Flash is used heavily on video websites such as You Tube, Hulu, MetaCafe, and Daily Motion. Most of the time, it works great, but when it does malfunction, users may not be able to view the content they enjoy most. When flash does malfunction, they can see anything from a blank spot on the web page to an error message stating, "Hello, you either have JavaScript turned off or an old version of Macromedia's Flash Player. Get the latest Flash player." When this happens, many people go through the process of uninstalling and reinstalling flash only to find the same problems.

Most of the time, much frustration can be eliminated by uninstalling Flash player using, "Adobe Flash Uninstaller." This program is available at the following sources:

http://download.macromedia.com/pub/flashplayer/current/uninstall_flash_player.exe
for Microsoft Windows

http://download.macromedia.com/pub/flash/ts/uninstall_flash_player.hqx for Mac OS 8.x-9.x

http://download.macromedia.com/pub/flash/ts/uninstall_flash_player_osx_10.2.dmg for Mac OS 10.2 and lower

http://fpdownload.macromedia.com/get/flashplayer/current/uninstall_flash_player_osx.dmg for Mac OS 10.3 and higher

Another very frustrating problem that

can occur is when Microsoft's .NET suite malfunctions. While most users do not directly interact with the .Net suite, many programs depend upon .NET to function. Most of the time, when such a program fails to function due to .NET, there will be an error message related to .NET. Many times using the uninstall tool that is found in the Add/Remove programs will not solve the problem. This is where ".NET Framework Cleanup Utility" may come to the rescue. This program has the option of removing .NET completely from the computer. It removes all traces left by the official .NET tool. This program can be downloaded for free from http://cid-27e6a35d1a492af7.skydrive.live.com/self.aspx/Blog_Tools/dotnetfx_cleanup_tool.zip

One of the very best general

uninstaller programs that will uninstall just about any program on a Windows computer is called "Revo Uninstaller." This program has even been used to uninstall malicious software such as the common fake antivirus programs that take over computers. It will uninstall programs even when the computer is running in what is called "Safe Mode" Revo Uninstaller is available from

http://www.revouninstaller.com/start_freeware_download.html.

Another program that can take care of frustrating problems that send computers to the shop is called "Quick Fix." It solves problems such as, Task Manager being disabled, no command prompt, disabled registry editor, no folder options, missing CD/DVD drive, slow menus, slow shutdowns, disabled control panel, disabled display properties as well as many other problems. Quick Fix can be downloaded from the following locations:

http://www.softpedia.com/progDownload/XP-Quick-Fix-Download-134770.html for Windows XP

http://download.cnet.com/7-Quick-Fix/3000-2094_4-75024066.html?part=dl-10055425&subj=dl&tag=button for Windows Vista and Windows 7

<u>Hardware</u>

Hardware is the tangible parts of a computer. It is the electronics, chassis, wires, keyboard, etc. Hardware is generally cheap and reliable. However, like everything else, it can fail and does wear out.

Below is information on how to

maintain it for long periods of use as well as some things that can be tried in order to find out what is wrong and how to fix it should things go wrong. When a computer has normally worked but has suddenly stopped after transport, the usual culprit is a loose connection on the motherboard or interconnecting wiring. The user should disconnect power, grasp or firmly touch the metal part of the computer chassis, and gently push down and re-seat each card in the computer and check to make sure each memory chip is properly seated. The user should also check to make sure each power connector is also properly seated. Doing this can save a trip to the repair shop as well as the bill. This is mentioned in the introductory paragraph because it is such a common problem and should be the very first thing checked.

Cleaning

Dust and dirt are the biggest enemies of a computer. Dust can build up quickly over a period of a few months. Computers should be checked for dust at least once every few months. The dust can be vacuumed out with a good vacuum cleaner or blown out with canned or compressed air.

Power Supply

The power supply in a computer provides exactly what its name implies, power to the computer and the hardware within. When a computer will not start up or show any form of startup screen, the power supply is one of the first things to check. The easiest and most reliable way to check a power supply on a computer is to unplug the computer, disconnect the power supply connections from the computer, and connect a known working power supply. The good thing about this is the fact that most any computer power supply is electrically equivalent to other power computer supplies. What this means is that a person does not have to mount the power supply in the computer itself. He or she only has to plug the power supply connections to the motherboard and drive devices.

If the computer uses cooling shrouds to direct air from the power supply fan to the processor (or other) heat sink, then it is highly recommended that an external fan be directed at the same heat sink in order to prevent overheating. If all connections are made, and the computer starts up normally, then this is a very reliable indicator that the power supply in the computer is malfunctioning, and it should be replaced.

Motherboard

The motherboard is the "brains" of the computer. There are many things that can go wrong with the motherboard that causes lockups, blue screens (kernel panics for non Microsoft operating systems), reboots, and non functioning peripherals. For the purposes of this book, the processor, memory, and any other component that resides upon the motherboard even though it is easily removable will be considered a part of the motherboard. This includes plug in PCI and proprietary add on cards. If a computer will not boot up or make it to the operating system splash or boot-up screen, a primary suspect is the motherboard, power supply, and hard drive. If the power supply is swapped out with a known good power supply, then it becomes fairly simple to eliminate other systems.

There are several ways to test a motherboard. The first goal is to at least try to make it to the splash screen for the computer. This is the screen that displays the computer or motherboard's hardware branding. If a computer stopped booting up after transporting it, then a loose connection or loosely seated memory chip or a mis seated peripheral card should be suspected.

If the computer is turned on and all is heard are beeps coming from the computer, then the motherboard is emitting an error condition signal. This signal is meant to give the technician a clue as to what is going on. A good way to interpret the beep sequences is to get on the Internet and type in the model number of the computer or motherboard and then the words, "POST beep." A visit to a good general site that covers this is http://www.bioscentral.com. Once the beeps are properly looked up, corrective action can be taken.

If there are no beeps emitted from the motherboard, the computer should be unplugged and all connections checked. Once this is done, the computer may be plugged in and retested. If the computer still does not boot up, the computer should be unplugged and all peripheral (PCI) cards should be removed. If the computer then boots up, then one of the cards is suspect. The computer can be unplugged and each card re-inserted one at a time to determine which one is suspect.

The same thing should also be done with internal hard drives, floppy, and any CD or DVD drive. If the computer still does not boot up, then it should be unplugged and the CMOS battery should be removed. If the computer is a notebook or laptop computer, then the battery should be removed as well. Once this is done, the computer should be left alone for about 10 minutes, the CMOS battery reinstalled and the computer should be plugged back in. If the computer is a laptop, the battery should also be re-installed before the computer is plugged in. If the computer boots up, then the problem is likely a bad battery or the BIOS became corrupted. After all of these things have been tried, then the problem is likely a motherboard, processor, or memory chip issue. If available, other known good memory modules (and processors) can be tried.

If the problem results in computer

lockups or rebooting, then it is time to determine whether the problem is software (operating system) or hardware related. This can be determined by loading a CD or USB based operating system such as Linux. Such operating systems are available for free on line.

Storage

Hard disk drives, for the most part, are electromechanical devices and can wear out. Even solid state devices such as thumb drives also have a limited number of times each sector can be written. Due to these facts, it is important to maintain a backup of all important files.

Sometimes, even if a hard disk does go bad, it may still be possible to recover some files that are stored on it. This can be done by placing the hard drive in an anti-static bag and storing it in a freezer for a day or two. After the drive reaches the temperature in the freezer, it should be immediately connected to a computer as a secondary drive and the attempt to recover files should be done as quickly as possible.

Technical Support

There are many cases where someone may call on another person to help them with a problem with a technological problem. Much frustration can be eliminated with a couple of tools available. These include a problem database as well as a screen shot database. These provide the person giving support handy references to make the troubleshooting process easier. Another solution is to use the free remote assistance and login programs that are also discussed in the next chapter this book.

There are many place on-line to get free technical help with computer related problems. Some sites include:

http://www.bleepingcomputer.com   Computer support for novice computer users

http://www.hddguru.com
Information, software, and help for problems specifically related to hard disk drives and other storage mediums

http://www.modemhelp.com   Help with telephone modems and dial up Internet issues.

http://www.technibble.com   A website for technicians and do it yourself-ers by technicians.

Many people who work with computers and have established themselves as knowledgeable find themselves walking others through fixes on the phone. This can be difficult in some cases unless there is a visual reference in front of the person giving the advice. Others may need this visual reference in order to follow instructions. The good news is the fact that there are plenty of visual references called "screenshots" available online. URL's to screenshot databases are listed below:

Microsoft Operating Systems

Windows XP

http://screenshots.modemhelp.net,
http://screenshots.leeindy.com

Windows Vista

http://screenshots.modemhelp.ne
t

Router Setup:

Linksys WRT-54G

http://screenshots.leeindy.com/lin
ksys_login.shtml

Chapter 2 - Remote Access

Remote access software allows someone to access their computer via Internet instead of having to travel to the location of the computer. A good remote access program allows a person to see the remote computer's desktop as if he or she is sitting right in front of it. There are several remote access software packages that are subscription based. The subscription costs usually are monthly recurring costs. The good news is that there are also free programs that accomplish the same thing without the monthly fee. These are listed below. If after reading this, one decides to use Logmein or UltraVNC, or any on the other free remote access programs instead of Gotomypc.com, then this book has already paid for itself.

LogMeIn

LogMeIn is a combination of a website and a program. To use Logmein to remotely control a computer, one needs to be at the computer to be controlled and download a program from https://secure.logmein.com/produ cts/free/. At the LogMeIn website, one can choose from many different types of accounts that can be used. For most people, the free account will suffice. The free version allows one to one log into and remotely control a computer on which the program is installed provided the computer is connected to the Internet. The professional version also offers the ability to transfer files between computers, print documents from the remote computer to a local printer, share files with others and more. Even with the free edition, one can still transfer files simply by using other programs on the remote computer. These programs that can be used to transfer files include email, ftp, or even chat and instant messaging programs. Even the simple web browser on the remote computer can be used to post on line and allow the local computer to download the file from the website. The remote computer (the one to be remotely controlled) needs to be already powered on in order to be controlled.

Show My PC

Another similar service is available from http://www.showmypc.com. Show My PC must be started each time it is to be used. The person who wishes to share the PC then enters his or her email address and generates a password. The email address and the generated password is then given out to users. The generated password is different than the password used on the email account or a least it should be. Users wishing to connect to the computer must supply the correct email address and password. Another good thing about Show My PC is the fact that it can be used on Microsoft Windows, Mac and Linux.

Team Viewer

Team Viewer is another remote control solution available for Windows, Mac, and Linux. It is free to use for non commercial purposes. In order to use Team Viewer, the person who wishes to share his or her computer starts the program. The program generates a session identification number as well as a session password . This information is then passed to the person who will be connection. The person connecting then opens the Team Viewer program and enters the session id and password in the box and connects. Team Viewer is available for download from http://www.teamviewer.com.

Ultra VNC

Ultra VNC is another program that allows one to remotely control computers over the Internet. While Ultra VNC allows more independence due to the fact that one does not have to depend upon a single central service to provide control, it is also much more difficult to set up. This is due to the fact that one has to manually set up their router to forward connections to the computer to be controlled. One also has to either have what is called a static IP address or use a service that allows a domain name to be associated to a dynamic (changing) IP address. Such a service is available through an organization called "DynDNS." The website to sign up for DynDNS is located   at http://www.dyndns.com. For the average computer user who desires remote control of their computer, Log Me In is recommended over using UltraVNC due to the easy setup.

Free Domains

Free domains are available through a service called DynDNS. DynDNS is a service that allows people with dynamic (changing) IP addresses to host their own web pages, email servers, and any other service that is typically provided by commercial hosting services.

http://www.dyndns.com is the website where one can actually choose from a number of free domains. Computers that are set up to use DynDNS usually have a program running on them that occasionally logs into the DynDNS host in order to keep the proper IP address updated. In fact, if updates do not occur frequently enough, DynDNS will send an email notice that notifies the user of the domain that their domain name will expire if an update is not performed soon.

http://www.asterisk.org

http://astbook.asteriskdocs.org

Chapter 3 - Telephony

Telephony or two way voice communications over the radio or wire has been around since the nineteenth century. Until the late last century, things remained under the control of monopolies. Since the break up of these monopolies, telephony and other electronic communication technologies have grown by leaps and bounds. This has allowed competition and also has given the consumer a wide variety of choices. Many forms of telephony are cheap and some are free, if one know where to look.

Internet Telephony

Internet telephony or V.O.I.P. (Voice Over Internet Protocol) is for the most part either extremely cheap or altogether entirely free. Internet telephony routes calls over the Internet. In order to take advantage of this service and have decent quality of service, a broadband connection such as cable, DSL, FIOS, or other equivalent low latency connection is needed. Broadband Internet via satellite usually does not qualify since there is extremely high latency and also due to the fact that satellite Internet companies also impose a maximum amount of data throughput each month of service. If a satellite communication method is used, one can expect portions of conversations to be lost, echoing during communications, etc. This is due to the high latency of the satellite connection.

Latency is the time it takes a packet of data to travel from its source to its destination. Latency in satellite communication is due to the long distance that a packet has to travel from earth to the satellite and back again. When using Internet telephony, one has to take the reliability of his or her Internet connection into consideration. V.O.I.P. communication is useless when an Internet connection on either end is down. One also should consider that not all V.O.I.P. providers provide 911 or emergency calling service. Some V.O.I.P. Services also provide video calling features. Some V.O.I.P. services require the use of a computer or computer like device while others allow the use of cheaply available analog terminal adapters. Each V.O.I.P. service can be classified as being open or proprietary as well. Open V.O.I.P. means that the service uses standard accepted communications protocols that are free to be used to integrate into independent communication devices or programs. Such protocols include SIP, SCCP (Skinny Client Control Protocol), MGCP (Media Gateway Control Protocol), Megaco H.248 (Gateway Control Protocol), IAX (Inter-Asterisk Exchange) among many others. It is usually not necessary to know the specifics of each and every one of these open protocols, but it can be important to be aware of the existence of the ones listed. Proprietary protocols are closed protocols that are used by specific services. Proprietary protocols are usually a closely guarded trade secret and are required to be licensed if used by other providers or device makers.

Proprietary protocols are an many cases free for the public to use as long as the public is using the service's program. Each type is discussed below is discussed in this chapter.

In addition to setting up Analog terminal adapters (Internet to regular telephone service) to connect to V.O.I.P services, it also may be necessary to configure any router to forward V.O.I.P packets to the correct device. If the subscriber of a V.O.I.P service decides to use connect his or her home's telephone wiring to distribute Internet phone service to all of the phone in the home, he or she will need to disconnect the telephone company's service from the wires used to distribute the V.O.I.P. service. This is usually not too difficult since most telephone company N.I.D.'s or phone boxes located on the outside of the home have a place where consumers can legally connect or disconnect wiring. In many cases, all that is required is for the user to unplug a plug. After the the home phone wiring is disconnected from the telephone company's line, the user simply plugs one end of a telephone cord into the Internet telephony device and the other end into the telephone jack. This should distribute the dial tone to the entire house.

In cases where the user desires to continue phone service with their local telephone company in addition to using Internet phone service, he or she can use the second pair of wires in the telephone wiring (if available and not in use). This second pair is usually colored yellow and black or white orange and orange white. If this second pair of wires are not connected, each wire can be connected to the other wire of the same color or color combination. Yellow should be connected to other yellow wires. Black wires should be connected to other black wires. The same thing applies to orange/white wires and white/orange wires. Care should be taken not to mix the two up. Once this is done, one can test the wiring by simply plugging one end a telephone cord from the V.O.I.P. (Internet Phone) device and the other end into a telephone plug. One also needs to use a 2 line telephone cord as well as a two line phone for this to work. If there is no dialtone, then the user needs to check to make sure the second line wires are connected inside the telephone jack.

One very popular V.O.I.P. service is called, "Skype." Skype allows a computer user to call other Skype users for free. Skype requires the use of the services' free to use but proprietary program. With a USB video camera (also known as a webcam) it is possible for one to make and receive voice calls that let caller and callee see each other as they talk. Skype not only works in the United States, but it also works all over the world. In addition to being able to reach other Skype users, Skype allows for the purchase of call credits that allow users to call regular telephones.

When a Skype user calls a regular telephone, the video option is not available. Skype can be downloaded at no cost by visiting http://www.skype.com. Skype does not necessarily require the use of a computer in order to be utilized. One can buy a device to convert the Skype communications protocol so that it will work with a regular phone. The device must not be required to be connected to a USB port. If the device requires connection to a USB port, then the computer must be on in order to use the device.

Skype uses a proprietary communications protocol, and any V.O.I.P. device meant to convert Internet telephone signals to a regular telephone service must specifically say that it works with Skype. Skype is a very popular program, and it is also recommended by the author. Skype runs on Windows, Apple operating systems, and Linux.

Another great V.O.I.P service that is available is called, Magic Jack. Magic Jack allows a user to buy a device that plugs into a USB port on a computer. The device contains software that allows the computer to install and set up service. Although Magic Jack does not include video chat or calling, it does allow one to plug in and use a regular telephone. In addition, Magic Jack also provides the subscriber with an incoming telephone number so that people can call the subscriber with a regular, cellular, or V.O.I.P. telephone. Magic Jack also allows 911 dialing to be configured and used although this service is not guaranteed. At the time of writing, Magic Jack uses an Open V.O.I.P. protocol called SIP. A sufficiently advanced computer user can monitor the computer connection on which Magic Jack is used and grab the SIP account name, password, and the I.P. address to which the Magic Jack program registers. Once this information is obtained, it can be entered into any generic SIP analog terminal adapter, and it will no longer be necessary to leave the computer on at all times.

Ooma is another service that provides cheap V.O.I.P. (phone via Internet) service. The website, http://www.ooma.com claims that the only thing a person must pay to use its service are "taxes and fees." Ooma service requires a small device which uses the standard SIP protocol with "custom extensions." Its service is also routed over a special connection called a VPN or virtual private network that connects a box sold by Ooma to to Ooma's computers. Even though the device incorporates a standard V.O.I.P communications method, the author considers the service as "proprietary" due to the fact that it uses a virtual private network as well as the fact that custom extensions and headers are utilized. Ooma allows subscribers to set up their own incoming local phone number as well as a traditional phone.

Other services include http://www.voipstreet.com, http://www.voip.ms, as well as many other competing services use open communication protocols. Some of them are set up for outgoing calls only while others provide options for setting up local telephone numbers (D.I.D. or direct inward dialing). These service allow standard S.I.P. devices available on-line to be used. These S.I.P devices allow regular telephones to be used for making and receiving calls. It is worth looking into these various Internet telephone services due to the fact that each different services sometimes offer capabilities not available to standard traditional or V.O.I.P end users. Being able to change what shows up on the Caller ID display of people who are called using this service is one example of extended capability.

The ability to change Caller ID information is something that has a few legitimate purposes such as allowing mental health counselors to call patients at home with the Caller ID information showing the number of the counseling agency. Another use is to allow business that have multiple lines to have their main number show up on the Caller ID displays of people with whom the company does business. A few V.O.I.P. providers even allow call recipients to be able to unmask the Caller ID information of calls where such information is blocked. This is a very handy tool for companies that receive large numbers of harassing calls. V.O.I.P. software and hardware can be integrated with traditional telephone equipment such as telephone systems used in large and small businesses.

In addition to installable software as well as hardware devices, there is also another way to make a few quick calls over the Internet by using a web browser to initiate the call. Several V.O.I.P. Providers allow calls to be initiated over the world wide web. These websites work by taking telephone number inputted by the user to make the call. The websites use V.O.I.P. To initiate a call to the number making the call. The website causes the calling person's phone to rings, and when the ringing phone is answered, the website then connects that call to the party being called. Websites that use this system include http://www.voipbuster.com and http://www.turbocall.com. With Voipbuster, when one makes a call he or she has to enter the country code for both the calling and called number in front of the called number. If the user is calling 1 (777) 777-7777 from 1 (666) 666-6666, He or she will enter +1666666666 in the "Your phone number" field and +17777777777 in the "Destination phone number" field. Turbocall works in a similar fashion, but a person has to register for an account before making calls.

There is one company in the United States that provides free telephone numbers in Washington state. Calls to a number issued by this company are routed to a computer specified by the user. The calls are routed via the open SIP protocol. The registration website for this company is http://www.ipkall.com . The computer to which calls are routed can be either a computer or SIP capable analog terminal adapter or even a SIP based telephone. Such a telephone number that when called routes calls to a computer is called a direct inward dial or (D.I.D). Most D.I.D.'s cost some money, but then again, some, like IPKall, are free.

Many other countries also offer direct inward dial or virtual telephone numbers. If a person has access to a computer and a high speed Internet connection, he or she can set up a D.I.D. in a country where family or friends may not have access to high speed Internet. If set up correctly, the friend can then call the user without having to pay exorbitant international rates. One needs only to search on-line for "free D.I.D." in order to find companies that offer that offer free or cheap D.I.D.'s in other countries.

One way for callers to save money is for them to use Google Voice. Google voice allows a person to obtain a free local number that is forwarded to another telephone number. One use for this is to allow a person to set up a local number in a different area and have any calls to that number routed to another telephone number in a different area. A person can set up a local telephone number in Lafayette, Louisiana and have any calls to that number forwarded to Panama city, Florida. This allows the caller in Lafayette to dial a local number and reach a person in Panama City without having to shell out money for a long distance call. Another way this can be used is for a person to get a number local to him or her and set the number so that rings a number in a distant area. The person to whom the number is routed will have to enter a verification number when Google call him or her to verify the set up. This verification code can be given in an instant message. This option is good for people who are stuck with dial up Internet. The website for Google voice is https://www.google.com/voice.

There is another service that is called Vonage that allows one to use his or her broadband Internet to provide home phone service. It too, allows the subscriber to pick an available incoming telephone number. However, Vonage is relatively expensive compared to other V.O.I.P. options and has a proprietary protocol and therefore is not discussed further. However, people interested in this service can visit http://www.vonage.com for pricing and other information.

Voice Mail, IVR, and Automatic Call Screening

Voice mail, IVR, and Automatic Call Screening are provided by many different programs and devices. Unfortunately, most of these are extremely expensive. However, there is one good free one that works extremely well, and it is called, "Asterisk." Asterisk is what is called a Private Branch Exchange program. A private branch exchange (PBX) is like a miniature telephone company. It provides a dial tone to phones, connects phones to other phones when their number is dialed, and it rings a phone when it receives an incoming call. Not only does it provide basic phone service, it can also be configured to provide extras such as call waiting, Caller ID, call screening, voice mail, and an aggravating phone tree much like one would hear when one needs to call a big company with a question or billing dispute. However, when connecting a computer running the Asterisk phone system with the traditional phone service, an inexpensive device is needed. This device in known as a FXS or foreign exchange station. It needs to convert a traditional phone signal into a V.O.I.P. signal so that it can be processed by the computer. Such a device can be had for less than a hundred dollars per line. In fact, the author bought an eight port FXS for less than $200 on E-Bay. While Asterisk was originally written for Linux and other Unix variants, it can be run in Microsoft Windows as well. Asterisk is used in homes, small businesses, large businesses, and even call centers around the world. This is due to the fact that it is inexpensive to use and relatively simple to set up in comparison to many proprietary phone systems. Asterisk for Unix or Linux can be downloaded from http://www.asterisk.org/.

Asterisk for Windows requires the use of another program called a virtual machine. The good news is the fact that the virtual machine can be downloaded free of charge. Chapter six of this book covers this option. Asterisk is a highly capable and configurable program. It has the same and even greater capabilities as software packages costing tens of thousands of dollars. One of these capabilities include selective call routing based upon the Caller ID information of an incoming call. For example, a telemarketer or known scammer may receive a messages stating, "This number is disconnected or no longer in service. Please check the number and try your call again." A trusted friend calling in may receive a message, "Hi Lane, I'm away on vacation and will be back next Monday, will you please pick up my mail and check on my house on your way home from work." An important client who is not good at all at remembering or writing down telephone numbers may call in, and the call will be routed to the user's home phone, cellular phone, or all three might be rung. Another possible use may be for a family to have a cell phone for each member and want all the cell phones to ring when someone calls the home number. This can be easily done with the Asterisk program. Another use for Asterisk may be to set up a local number or use an already existing number to allow the user to call in and then dial out to to other phone networks such as Skype or other private phone networks.

Yet another use is for doctors, lawyers, psychologists to be able to call their clients and use it to show their work number instead of their home or cell phone number. Yet another money saving use is to use Asterisk to monitor an alarm system instead of paying a company such as A.D.T. or another alarm company. Asterisk can also be used to place outgoing calls, and in some cases, it can save small companies hundreds or thousands of dollars a month. If the company wants to communicate confidential trade secrets between different offices, Asterisk can be used to provide an encrypted connection so that eavesdroppers cannot steal information by listening to the call. Asterisk can also be used to place outgoing calls automatically or be set up to place wake up calls for businesses such as hotels.

Asterisk can also be used to provide telephone service to a few phones or thousands in a small or big business. The uses of Asterisk is limited only by the knowledge and imagination of the user. In order to use Asterisk, some reading is required. This is due to the fact that asterisk needs to be set up to work with V.O.I.P services and devices. It also has to be set up to correctly route and handle calls between the various devices and services. The good new is that there is an electronic book called, "Asterisk The Future of Telephony" that explains in pretty decent detail on how to set up Asterisk from beginning to end. Even better is the fact that the book is totally free in its electronic form and can be found at http://astbook.asteriskdocs.org/.

http://www.asteriskdocs.org provides free documentation and help for everyone from rank beginners to seasoned professionals. The detailed setup of Asterisk is beyond the scope of this book, but in keeping with the philosophy of this book, the author points the reader to the freely available information. It should also be noted that since Asterisk is a free program in terms of both distribution and the license to modify and redistribute, there are many different distributions (or custom software packages) of Asterisk. Some of these distributions allow the user to configure the software simply by entering account information and using point and click on a web page to actually route calls and handle calls.

Using and setting up the original Asterisk does require a little understanding of a few terms and concepts which are explained here. A few of the concepts include extensions, channels, trunks and dial plans. An extension is simply a number or name that is dialed or typed into a communication device. When someone dials a number on a phone, the number that was dialed is seen as an extension by the telephone company's computer.

With newer, fancier, and more high tech telephone or video communication devices, an extension may also include letters. A channel is the route taken by communications. A channel can be a simple telephone line, an Internet protocol (V.O.I.P) account, a T1 line, ISDN, radio link, or a cellular service. With the Asterisk telephone system, each type of channel has its own configuration file. This configuration file contains information that is needed in order to set up the channel. This information includes information on how to connect to the other end of the channel. Such information includes an Internet address (if applicable), user name, password, and any other needed information. Channel configuration files are usually simply named. File names are sip.conf for the

SIP protocol, iax.conf for the inter asterisk protocol, etc. The term channel and trunk is used interchangeably. They are synonymous. Another thing critical for the operation of the Asterisk program is what is called a dial plan. A dial plan simply instructs Asterisk on how to route and handle calls. A dial plan may look complicated at first, but once the concept is understood, it becomes much easier. Asterisk's dial plan is stored in a file extensions.conf. The details of channel configuration and dial plan files are summarized here.

If Asterisk is located on a local area network that is connected to the Internet via a router, then it will be necessary to set up port forwarding to forward incoming Internet traffic to the correct ports on the router. Ports 5060 and 5061 on the Internet side of the router needs to be forwarded to the computer on which Asterisk is installed. In addition, the computer on which Asterisk is installed should be set up to use a static (never changing) IP address.

Prepaid Cell Phone Service

Pre-paid cell phone service has for years suffered the stigma of being for those who are unqualified to subscribe to a contract phone due to poor credit. For years, it has also been high priced with poor quality phones and bad coverage.

However, things are rapidly changing. The cost of a prepaid cell phone subscriptions have dropped tremendously. In addition, the quality of phones as well as services have improved until they are now on par with the contract carriers. In addition, prepaid telephone services are more accountable to customers due to the fact that customers can drop the carrier at any time without penalty. This is not the case with contract providers, but there are ways to drop them without penalty as well. This will be discussed later on.

For people who use their cell phones for mainly calling and texting may find that prepaid is the way to go. There are several different companies offering prepaid cell phone service. For most pre-paid cellular services, it is necessary to buy a phone set up to work with the service. The subscriber must buy a certain number of minutes within a certain period of time. Minutes are usually purchased by buying a card with the number of minutes listed on the card. The user must scratch off a small section of the card in order to reveal a number. This number is entered into the phone, and the minutes usually show up shortly thereafter. Some services offer monthly plans as well. For people who do not use the phone very often, the card option is probably the best choice.

Tracfone is one of the most popular prepaid cell phone service. Tracfone is the service used by the author. Tracfone offers either a monthly plan or a per minute plan. In order to add minutes to a phone, a card must be purchased to do so. In addition, a special card can be purchased that will double any minutes on subsequent cards. Even better, there is another card that can be purchased that will both double the minutes of any card purchased thereafter and will also make the minutes last for a year. When one enters the card number into the phone, he or she is also given a chance to enter a promotional code in order to get free additional minutes.

However, it is best to register for a free account with the Tracfone website and use this account to add minutes to the phone when using promotional codes. This is due to the fact that if a specific code does not work or there is an error while entering the code, the website gives the user a chance to try again or to enter another code. When the code is not accepted directly on the phone, the minutes are added without the chance to re-enter the promotional code. Tracfone uses promotional codes for several reasons including clearing out old phone inventories. Many times, promotional codes were shipped in coupon inside the packaging of clearance phone.

People get these phones and add the codes to the various coupon website in order to pass saving to fellow subscribers. Promotional codes can be looked up on-line at several websites including

http://preprepaid.com/currenttracfonebonus.php,

http://www.retailmenot.com/view/tracfone.com,

http://www.fone-review.com/TracFone_Promotional_Codes.html,

http://www.tracfone.com, and many others. One disadvantage to Tracfone is the fact that Tracfone has a lock on any new feature additions such as ring tones and applications. These must be purchased from Tracfone.

Virgin Mobile is another very popular prepaid phone provider. Virgin Mobile also offers a pay as you go or a monthly service plan. It too allows the use of promotional codes when activating a phone or adding minutes. Some websites where these codes can be found include

http://www.promotioncode.org/VirginMobileUSA and http://www.retailmenot.com/view/virginmobileusa.com.

Unfortunately, Virgin Mobile's promotion code do not work as reliably as Tracfones. But, there are other benefits with using Virgin Mobile, especially for those who like phones packed with features. Virgin Mobile is more popular with the tech-savvy crowd simply because of additional features and services options such as unlimited messaging, texting, web browsing, etc. Virgin Mobile also has a large selection of smart phones . These smart phone include those running the Android operating system, Black Berries, etc. Many Virgin Mobile phones are also capable of connecting to the Internet via WIFI. This means that these phones are capable of making V.O.I.P phone calls over a WIFI local hotspot (providing access is not blocked by the WIFI provider) thereby conserving minutes on the phone. It is worth a look at Virgin Mobile's website, http://www.virginmobile.com, to see their big selection of smart phones. Virgin Mobile not only offers cheap phone service, but they also offer prepaid wireless Internet that is available anywhere there is Sprint coverage.

In addition to these two great prepaid cellular providers, there are many more. In fact, many of the contract providers are getting into the business of offering prepaid service. The websites below list some of the prepaid options.

http://www.wireless.att.com/cell-phone-service/go-phones/index.jsp

http://www.boostmobile.com

http://www.mycricket.com

http://www.consumercellular.com

http://www.commoncentsmobile.com

http://www.earthtones.com

http://www.kajeet.com/4u/index.html

http://www.greatcall.com/Affiliates

http://www.libertywireless.com

http://www.metropcs.com

http://www.net10.com

http://www.pagepluscellular.com

http://www.h2owirelessnow.com

http://www.platinumtel.com

http://www.readymobile.com

http://www.redpocketmobile.com
Caters to people who have family or contacts in Asia Pacific Island areas

http://www.stimobile.com/

http://www.straighttalk.com/

http://www.mysimplemobile.com
Allows customers to use their
unlocked GSM mobile phones.

http://www.t-
mobile.com/shop/phones/prepaid.
aspx

http://www.tracfone.com

http://www.totalcallmobile.com
has cheap calling to Mexico.
http://www.uscellular.com/uscellu
lar/zipCode.jsp?type=plans&plan-
selector-type=prepaid

http://venturemobile.com/store/z/

http://www.verizonwireless.com/b
2c/splash/prepay.jsp

http://www.virginmobileusa.com
caters to those who like feature rich

phones as well as those needing wireless Internet access plans

Make Ringtones

Many cell phone subscribers like to use customized ring tones. Ring tones are audio files that play when a call is received. There are many sites that allow such ring tones to be downloaded to phones. However, many of these sites require the user to pay subscription charges, or in the cases of "free" ring tones, they may spam the phone subscriber with unwanted text messages. Some sites that allow users to create their own free ring tones include

http://audiko.net/
and
http://makeownringtone.com/

One just follows the instructions on

the website to create the ring tones and then download the ring tone to the computer. After that, the ring tone can be emailed to the phone.

Chapter 4 Entertainment and Education

The Internet is a wonderful technology that has revolutionized the flow of information, entertainment, and political views. The Internet is the modern day equivalent of the printing press, radio, and television all rolled into one. Various free sites provide all of these things on line without costing a dime. How and if one can access these sites is determined by one's Internet providers.

Most cable and DSL Internet connections have liberal if any band width usage limits. This, unfortunately is not the case with satellite or some cell phone networks. Before signing up with an Internet service provider, one should research the terms and conditions of any contract. Some contracts may stick a person with a high priced and unreliable Internet service for years.

Internet TV

Cable and other pay TV services are losing subscribers due to the Internet. Free Internet TV tsites such as http://www.hulu.com allow people to watch television over the Internet while not having to pay subscribers fees.

Most of these sites are supported by advertising. This is not that different from free over the air television channels except for the price. Cable companies once offered the advantage of offing a clearer signal and fewer commercials. This, however, is no longer always the case. With cable and satellite providers such as Dish Network, most channels constantly interrupt programming with annoying and sometimes offensive commercials. These commercials are in many cases played much louder than the program. These commercials are in addition to the high subscriber fees charged by providers. Watching a few commercials and not having to pay the fees is a good motivation to get television on- line.

With all of the advantages of over the Internet TV, there are also a few disadvantages. Some but not all on line television services require the download and use of programs provided by the service. Some of these programs also install programs that display advertisements on the computer. Some of these programs also may allow malicious software to be downloaded to the user's computer as well. Some allow the user to use programs already installed on the computer. However, some of these services will prompt the user to download what is called a codec in order to view programming.

A codec (stands for coder decoder) is circuitry or software that converts data from one format to another. In the cases where a user is prompted to download a codec, the user is being asked to download software (computer instructions), Some of this software also carries adware or instructs the computer to download other forms of software including ad-ware. For other TV services, in order to view content, a site may require the user to link to his or her Facebook account. Since this will allow Facebook to track even more habits, the use of a separate Facebook account specially created for this purpose is recommended. Some

Internet TV and video services require registration to use. When forced to register, one can use an email address created specifically for this purpose. Some of the many TV and video sites include http://www.youtube.com, http://justin.tv, http://www.hulu.com, http://www.streamick.com, and http://www.worldtvpc.com.

One popular pay to stream TV service is known as Netflix. Netflix allows the streaming of movies and TV episodes via computer (Using Microsoft Windows), Nintendo Wii, Sony PS3, Microsoft X-box 360, iPad, and iPhone. Netflix will also work with TiVO, Roku, Logitekch Revue (with Google TV), many Internet connected Blue Ray Players as well as other devices. The cost is $7.99 per month. The nice part about Netflix is the fact that it offers a free 1 month trial in order to learn how to use the service and to get devices connected. While one has to pay for Netflix, it is much cheaper than cable or satellite, and at the time this is written, there is no streaming of news channels. It is worthwhile to visit http://www.netflix.com and see what it is all about. Getting Netflix to play on different devices is usually very simple.

On the PS3, simply select the PlayStation Network section of the main menu and install Netflix from the "What's New" area and follow the instructions on screen. On the Wii, select Netflix in the Wii Shop and follow the on screen instruction on how to connect via the Netflix Account. In order to watch on the Xbox 360, an Xbox LIVE Gold membership account is required. Simply go to the Video Marketplace, select Netflix, and follow the instructions from there. Other devices should have instructions on how to connect to Netflix.

Internet Radio

Just as there are plenty of sites on-line offering free and low cost television, there are also plenty of radio shows available on-line. Many website offer streaming radio services for free. Some of these sites are listed below:

http://www.jango.com

http://www.live365.com/index.html

http://www.shoutcast.com

For people who like to listen to talk shows and other less well known radio hosts, a good option is http://www.podfeed.net, or one can use a search engine to find their material. For example, to search for Michael Savage's show, one can go to Google and type in *"Michael Savage" podcast.* Programs such as Audacity (http://audacity.sourceforge.net) can be used to record the streaming audio and save it to disk. Firefox also has an extension called, "Download Helper" available at http://www.downloadhelper.net/ that will allow users to save streaming audio and other media from many Internet Radio stations and video websites. Files can be either burned to CD's for use in the car or downloaded to a mp3 player.

Books On-line

The Internet has made it easy for many people to publish books in an electronic format. The most popular file format for book is the PDF or Portable Document Format. In order to read a book in the pdf format, a program capable of reading the format needs to be used.

Fortunately, many such programs that can do so are available for free on-line. The most popular of these programs can be downloaded from http://www.adobe.com. Once this page is opened, the user should look to the right side of the page and click on, "Get Adobe Reader." When the next page opens, the user should click on the "Download now" link and follow the directions supplied.

Most books can be found easily on-line. Many e-books can be downloaded for free. Discussed here are several sites that have totally free, mixed free and paid books, and those that are pay only.

Most can be downloaded in the popular pdf format. Many books can also be downloaded by searching http://www.google.com. For example to search for the book, "Asterisk The future of Telephony," one can go to Google and type the following into the search box, *"Asterisk the Future of Telephony "filetype:pdf* (yes, the quotes are included). One place where books can be freely downloaded is http://www.gutenberg.org. The Gutenberg website has books who's copyrights have expired or which have been released for free. Another free book site is http://www.manybooks.net. This site specializes in books released under the Creative Commons license. A site that contains a mixture of both free books and books for sale is http://www.scribd.com. A site that specializes in free technical books is

Free On-line courses

When someone says that they want an education, one has to clarify what they mean. Do they actually mean that they want to learn about a specific subject or profession, or are they just seeking credentials so that they will be allowed to get a professional license or be accepted for employment in a particular field? It is also possible that they mean both. There are free courses on-line that provide for education, but unfortunately, these do not provide credentials or college course credit. Colleges and universities have become a huge money making industry, and their degrees are becoming more and more a mandate for success.

In many cases, despite having a degree, many college graduates are unsuccessful in maintaining employment due to the fact that even though they have studied a subject, they are not taught the tricks of the trade so to speak. This is especially true when these graduates work for small businesses. Many students are taught how to do things in a specific way and with specific equipment. They may not know how to adapt when such equipment is not available or when the business does a job differently than what was taught in school. This is a common problem among college graduates. In fact, a large percentage of college graduates end up working in a field that is different than their major area of study.

However, this is usually not the case for someone who has experience in a field and goes to college simply to get the credentials that companies and government require for advancement and hiring.

Those who are looking for an education in order to expand knowledge can do so without enrolling in college and universities. They can get this knowledge by reading books, watching videos and asking questions of people already involved in the field of study in which they are interested. This is how the author has learned the majority of what he knows. Skills related to a field can be obtained by simple practice. This is how skills have been obtained for many years.

Unfortunately, self-obtained knowledge is usually not respected by most big companies or governments. Someone who obtains knowledge, skill, and understanding in the self obtained manner has to prove him or herself in order to be taken seriously. There are several ways of doing this. One can work for someone who has credentials or start his or her own business or service. Another way to prove expertise is by writing a book, getting published in trade or professional journals, certification organizations, or by word of mouth.

Some college and universities offer free on-line courses. A list of these courses as well as courses from private entities can be obtained from the following sources:

http://www.docnmail.com

http://www.free-ed.net

http://www.openculture.com/free onlinecourses

Educational materials can also be obtained by downloading e-books as discussed earlier in this chapter. Those seeking to obtain credentials such as college degrees may still use the Internet to fulfill much of the requirements for a college degree. Instead of taking a course, the degree candidate takes a test. The commonly used tests to determine whether college credit is awarded are the CLEP (College Level Examination Program) and the DSST (Dantes Subject Standardized Test). Before going through the trouble of actually downloading and studying course textbooks, it is a good idea to find out how much credit by examination a particular college or university accept. Colleges have become a money making racket, so many are limiting the amount of transfer credits, credits by examination, etc, so that they can be sure to "get theirs."

In order to get credit by examination, one must find the college or university in which he or she wants to enroll, study the course outlines, obtain the course textbooks, and then start studying. Many of the textbooks for colleges and universities are available on-line and in electronic format. It is important to use the textbooks that the college or university uses in order to know what answers are expected. There are some good websites to visit to get free study materials for the C.L.E.P. Some are listed below:

http://www.collegeboard.com/student/testing/clep/about.html

http://educationcenter.dc.gov/ec/cwp/view,a,1307,q,581423.asp

http://www.nelnetsolutions.com/terc/

Dating

For many people, finding a good spouse is as important as a good education. Many people do find their significant other on-line. There are many different matchmaking and dating sites on line. Most comes with monthly or annual charges. However, some are also completely free and come with plenty of other users from whom to select a potential friend, spouse, etc. Five of the most popular free dating sites include

http://www.datehookup.com,

http://www.okcupid.com,

http://www.plentyoffish.com,

http://www.tagged.com,

and

http://www.zoosk.com,

While some people use dating sites to find mates, many others do the same using social networking sites such as http://www.myspace.com and

http://www.facebook.com.

Piracy

The author of this book in no way condones or recommends piracy. Piracy not only can cost huge corporations money, but it also can take rightfully earned money out of the hands of the independent writer, video producer or musician.

Industry and government claims that piracy is a big problem on the Internet. Piracy is the duplication and use of computer programs, movies, music, books, and other media without authorization. Downloading and using the free programs and services in this book is not considered piracy because the producers of these are releasing these for free use. Some of the programs must be downloaded directly from the producers' website while other may be freely distributed by any website.

People pirate media for several reasons. Some don't want to pay the asking price for the material. Some want to try before they buy, and some do it just for the fun of it.

There are several different organizations that combat piracy. These include the Business Software Alliance (B.S.A.) for software, the Recording Industry of America (R.I.A.A.) for audio recordings, the

Motion Picture Association of America (M.P.A.A.) for video content among many others. Once one of these organizations set their sights on someone they suspect that is violating copyright, they can become pretty ruthless. They have enough money to drag a case through the courts bankrupting their target simply through legal fees needed for defense. Hopefully, legislation will be passed that will protect people from draconian lawsuits and penalties in the near future. These organizations have caused innocent people untold misery. Copyright is a complex issue that is ripe for abuse on both side of the copyright argument.

Copyright and patents refer to a temporary government protected monopoly given to authors, inventors, and others who produce intellectual property. Many of the "public awareness" programs conducted by anti piracy organizations such as the Recording Industry Association of America, Motion Picture Association of America, and the Business Software alliance refer to the unauthorized copying and distribution of media as stealing. Stealing is the unauthorized removal of property which deprives the owner of said property. With piracy, the owner still has the property and the use of it. The person making a copy has simply made a copy. What pirates do is copyright infringement. Copyright infringement is violating the temporary given government monopoly on product distribution.

There are many different dangers related to copyright infringement. They range from lawsuits, "settlement offers," malicious software, to even time in prison for pirate who sell the illegally copied product. Federal legislation provides for exorbitant and excess damage awards for copyright infringement. One of the biggest consequences of copyright infringement is the fact that people or companies who do not get a big enough return on their investment in time and money creating media may end up going out of business or stop production. Even though this is the case, there are millions who still choose to commit copyright infringement. There are several reasons why people choose to engage in piracy. These include the fact that the desired material may no longer be found in stores, the price of the desired material is too high for the person committing the copyright infringement, the copyright infringer may want to try the content before buying, the pirated material may be stripped of annoying advertisements, interruptions, etc. The infringer may be protesting the draconian actions of the company holding the copyright, the extremely low odds of getting caught, or the infringer may be doing it just for fun. Copyright infringement is not solely the fault of the people doing the infringement, it is also the fault of companies and governments which have increased the terms of a copyright to such a period of time that the monopoly on copyrighted material is in effect forever.

Copyright infringement will continue as long as there is such a thing as copyright. This will be the case no matter what technology is employed to prevent it. This is due to the fact that if something can be seen or heard, it can be copied or imitated.

Grey areas

Grey areas in piracy or copyright infringement are those areas not clearly defined by the government, courts or various agencies which enforce copyright or prosecute copyright infringers.

There are several grey areas when it comes to piracy. These include recording the streaming audio from a recording label's website, using audio from a website's video, using a program to store a streaming audio or video, and CD or DVD ripping.

Other grey areas include the transferring of purchased media to another device or format, using software to make a backup of purchased media, and downloading content to replace destroyed media (scratched or cracked CD'S or DVD'S).

Alternatives to Piracy

Piracy has had a positive impact for consumers of content. It has given the customer leverage when it comes to the purchase of media. The Internet and other technology has opened distribution channels for all forms of entertainment, information, and other media like no other means in the history of mankind. No longer do big business and big government control who publishes what content or who consumes what content. With modern technology, just about anyone can be a published author, musician, software developer, or movie producer. The author of this book has released several how to videos on the Internet for free. These videos provide the same information that is found in many expensive how-to videos sold by various outfits. The best part about the author's video's is the fact that they are free for the download. This is the case with many content producers. Free software can be found on-line at many different websites. The author highly recommends http://www.sourceforge.net. Video can also be found at many sites for free as well.

http://www.youtube.com is just one example. Other examples are listed in a previous chapter.

Music is also available for free on-line. Many bands and musicians both well known and not so well known have published their music on their websites, social network profiles, or on sited dedicated to the publishing of free music. The nice part about this is the fact that people can find the exact music to suit their taste. While one may run across lousy music, in many cases the music is of equal and better quality than what is sold by the stores or big music. Like it or not, the big media, publishers and software companies now have to face competition. This has in many cases resulted in lower prices and better quality.

Cable companies are losing subscribers to on-line competition,and so are satellite TV companies. Book publishers and newspapers are also facing steep competitions. Some companies will be stubborn and keep their prices at the same level as were previously borne by customers, and some will adapt and lower their prices to reflect the new reality. Many record labels and music stores have hit upon hard times due to the fact that they charge greater than $15 for the same content that is available on-line for 99 cents or even free.

Most of their remaining customers are

unaware of the availability of the same content on-line or do not know how to obtain this content on-line. Most people are willing to pay for what they use, but they are not willing to be ripped off. Why should they pay 50 to 100 dollars each month for a cable subscription when they can watch the same content on-line for free or subscribe to cheap service such as Netflix (http://www.netflix.com)? The author has noticed cable and satellite companies moving in the right direction by offering free viewing for premium channels for limited times, deals to entice new customers. Those reading this book can use their knowledge to get a better deal from their pay television providers by mentioning the competition as well as the much lower prices. It is not necessary to resort to piracy in order to avoid being ripped off, but it is nice to know where to find the deals.

Types of File Sharing software

File sharing software is also known as peer to peer software. Peer to peer file sharing means sending files to and receiving files from other computers on a network (such as the Internet). The term peer is used to denote the fact that the other computer is just a regular computer not normally set up to serve web pages, email, news, or other services where people log on. In other words, the peer is not normally a website such as www.walmart.com or www.google.com, etc. There are several types of peer to peer protocols (methods of communications and file transfer), and each one is generally used for a specific type of content. The protocols are the actual methods of transfer and have different names from the programs that use them.

Gnutella is a protocol that is popular for sharing music and documents. It can also be used for video, but many purported video file listed are spam videos. This is especially true for the file type, mov.

Bitorrent is a protocol that is used to share videos, entire CD's, DVD's, and software packages. It is also sometimes used to share documents as well. These two protocols are the most popular on-line today.

The most popular filesharing software that uses the above protocols are Frostwire for the Gnutella protocol and Vuze for the Bittorrent protocol. Both require Java to be installed. However, the good new is the fact that Java is freely downloadable from http://www.java.com. Once Java is downloaded and installed, one can then install Frostwire and Vuze.

Frostwire can be downloaded by visiting http://www.frostwire.com.
Frostwire allows the user to search for the music, documents, pictures or video by typing in the title of the material sought. FrostWire is mainly used for downloading individual songs. When using Frostwire one selects the type of file being sought (audio, images, video, documents, programs, or all types), types in the title or name of the software, and then clicks on the search button. In the search results window, there will be a list of all files found. When deciding to download a file, one should pay attention to the what is listed under the type column in order to prevent downloading malicious

software. For audio files, mp3 or wav files are the safest. For image files, jpg, bmp, tif, and gif files are the safest. For video files, avi files are one of the safest. For document files, txt is the safest.

When installing FrostWire, it is best to uncheck any option offering to search one's computer for files to be shared. This is to prevent the unintentional sharing of confidential files or the sharing of too many files. The more copyrighted files one shares, the higher probability one will be caught by copyright enforcement organizations. The author usually shares less than 5 files. Vuze is another popular file sharing program. Vuze can be downloaded by visiting http://www.vuze.com. With Vuze, one usually needs to search for what is called a torrent file (file extension ending in .torrent). This torrent file may list a system used to coordinate sharing (tracker) as well as computers which are sharing the file. This torrent file is dragged and dropped into Vuze's download window, and Vuze attempts to connect to computers listed in the torrent. Vuze also includes the capability for searching for torrent files within the application itself.

Legitimate Uses of File Sharing

File sharing programs and websites are not meant just for people to commit copyright infringement. They are also used to legitimately distribute media that is intended to be used for free. Many versions of Linux are distributed via bittorrent and other file sharing protocols. This is done in order to minimize bandwidth (data transfer) costs for the publisher. Bittorrent is also a good protocol to distribute videos of meetings and religious services. Another legal application for file sharing networks is to distribute works created for the public domain.

Don't get caught

The odds of getting into trouble for sharing copyrighted files are lower than being struck by lightning. Although this is the case, there is still the real possibility of getting caught. The highest chance of getting caught is by using college or university networks to share files over the Internet. Most colleges and universities are real sticklers for protecting corporate intellectual property. Many colleges and universities will cooperate with copyright enforcement organizations. For anyone trading copyrighted material, it is best not to use college networks to connect to peer to peer file sharing networks. For people who stay on college campuses, it is best to share material through physical means such as thumb drives, or DVD discs. In fact, this is the safest way to trade files in any other file sharing circumstance.

Alternatives to File Sharing Software

Programs such as Audacity (http://audacity.sourceforge.net) can be used to record streaming audio from the World Wide Web and save it to disk. Firefox also has an extension called, "Download Helper" available at http://www.downloadhelper.net/ that will allow users to save streaming audio and other media from many Internet Radio stations and video websites. These will help users save streaming audio and video content from websites they visit. This in turn saves people from having to connect to other users' computers in order to obtain content.

News reading software

Another option is called a newsgroup reader. Newsgroups or Usenet predates the world wide web and are still popular among hard core technophiles. In many cases, content that cannot be found anywhere else may be found on Usenet. Not all Internet service providers providers have Usenet servers set up for their subscribers. For those who fall into this category, a subscription to a newsgroup service is recommended. Another option is to search for *free newsgroup server* on a favorite search engine. Another place to look is http://freenews.maxbaud.net/.

Internet service providers who do host their own news servers usually name them something like news.myisp.net, nntp.myisp.net, news.yourisp.com, nntp.yourisp.com, or something very similar. One should contact his or her Internet service provider to see if their service does support newsgroups. Also required to read, download files, from, or even to list newsgroups is a program called a newsgroup or NNTP (Network News Transport Protocol) reader. One good program that is used by the author is called, "Pan." Pan can be downloaded from

http://pan.rebelbase.com/downlo ad/

Pan is free with no spyware or adware. It runs on both Windows and Linux. For movie, multimedia, or any large file download from newsgroups, it is best to search for nzb files. Nzb files are files that instruct a newsreader program as to what files need to be downloaded to complete a file. Nzb files can be found simply by searching (in Google, for example) for the desired file and adding filetype:nzb. A good example is if one is searching for Paint Plus, the terms typed into Google would be would be *"Paint Plus" filetype:nzb.* Once such a file is downloaded, the newsreader program needs to be opened and under file, either import nzb file will need to be selected or Open and then select nzb file depending on which newsreader is installed.

Backing up music and video

Many people who purchase DVD's and CD's wisely store their purchased material and use copies for everyday use. CD's can usually be copied directly to writable media while DVD's usually contain encrypted content and copy protection to prevent the same from happening. However, these can be copied with a program called DVDshrink. DVDshrink can be downloaded from many different sites. The creators of DVDshrink has a site called, http://www.dvdshrink.org. The program cannot be downloaded from their website due to restriction and legal issues. In other words, they don't want to risk being sued by big entertainment or having the site taken down. However, DVDshrink can be found by searching the web for DVDshrink. One place DVDshrink can be found is http://www.filehippo.com/download_dvdshrink.

The programs listed in this chapter provide great alternatives to using peer to peer programs in order to obtain content. They work simply because they are copying this content from websites where the content has already been uploaded. The author discourages piracy and only discuss it to educate users as to what programs are used to actually download copyrighted material.

Decompressing Archive Files

Many downloaded files are compressed so that they take less time to download. There are different types of archive files. One popular archive file format is zip archives. This type can be opened by a program such as winzip or unzip. Another very popular archive file format is rar archives. Both file formats can be opened with the free, open source program called, "7-zip" which is available at http://www.7-zip.org.

Chapter 5
On-line Publishing

The Internet is the modern day equivalent of the printing press, recording studio, book publisher, and television production company combined.

Documents

Documents can be created by many different programs. One of the best all round document program is called "OpenOffice." OpenOffice is free and compatible with Microsoft Office and can also export pdf files. Open Office can be obtained by visiting http://www.openoffice.org/.
Not only does Open Office allow the creation of text files but it also includes a spreadsheet, a Power Point like presentation program, and a program to access databases.

A good program for editing the graphics portion of a document is known as G.I.M.P. G.I.M.P. Is available at http://www.gimp.org.

Documents and books can be published on-line in many places and formats. No longer are authors and other content creators beholden to big media giants. In fact, many book which happen to turn out to be big sellers were initially rejected by traditional book publishers. The authors of these books resorted to self publishing and promotion and made out pretty well. There are several on-line sites that work to assist authors in getting published. Most of these do it for a share of the revenue. Websites of a few companies that help with publishing are listed in the publish on demand section later on in this chapter.

Those who want to publish their book themselves will find it very difficult to be heard above the noise of their competition. However, there are a few tricks that an author can use to make their product stand out, and these include giving some valuable information away for free while posting a link to their book's website or blog. When search engines scour the web, certain keywords related to topic in one's book will lead people to the author's website, and if the blog or website content is written well enough, sales will be generated. A short how to video posted on-line can contain a small advertisement or link to a book's website. This also works for many other products. It works even better if the video is entertaining. The more people who watch and like the video, the better chance of them visiting the producer's website.

Publish on Demand

Publish on demand is a newer service offered to authors and other content creators. For a per unit price, on demand publishing companies will print books or manufacture CD'S or DVD'S and in some cases, will send them to buyers freeing content authors from having to maintain inventory or invest in expensive printing or copying equipment. The content producer simply uploads their content to the publisher's website, and then notifies the publisher when media needs to be produced. Book publish on demand websites are listed here:

http://www.cafepress.com

http://www.createspace.com

(Provides free ISBN, but reports tax info to IRS)

Music and Video

Much entertainment and educational content is produced by small producers in the home or small business. Most of these producers do not have the multi thousands or million dollars necessary to be on national radio or TV. In many cases their content is produced with either pirated or free software. There are many high quality video and sound editing programs out there along with CD and DVD authoring or production software that produce quality videos. A couple of these are discussed in this chapter.

One popular sound editing program is called Audacity, Audacity allows a person to edit, record, and mix audio from different sources. It is available for Microsoft Windows, BSD, Mac OS X, and Linux. It can be downloaded from http://audacity.sourceforge.net. Http://www.youtube.com has plenty of instruction on how to use Audacity. All that has to be done is once http://www.youtube.com is loaded is to type in *Audacity* into the search box and click on Search. There are plenty of tutorials showing how to remove vocals from a music file, edit, input, and mix audio files.

For midi composition and editing Modplug Tracker is recommended. It can be downloaded from http://openmpt.org. Modplug tracker runs on Microsoft Windows and any platform that has the Wine windows emulator program installed. Like Audacity, there are also video tutorials on how to use Modplug Tracker available on You Tube.

Free video editing programs are also available. For Microsoft Windows, Windows Movie Maker is a free download from http://www.microsoft.com/windowsxp/downloads/updates/moviemaker2.mspx for Windows XP. Windows Live Movie Maker is available from http://explore.live.com/windows-live-movie-maker?os=other for Windows 7.

One very good program for video editing is known as Kdenlive. It contains the features that are found on professional products such as multi-track video time lines, multi-track audio, various transitions, various effects such as chroma key (also known as green screen). One of the best things about Kdenlive is that is is completely free and open source. Unfortunately, at this time, it only runs on BSD, Linux, and Mac OS X. However, using a virtualization program such as Virtual Box, it can be run under Linux as a guest operating system. Free virtualization is discussed in a chapter six this book. For those who want a professional grade video editing software who do not want to spend hundreds of dollars, going through the trouble of setting up Linux on a virtual machine is a worthwhile option. Video tutorials for using the video editors discussed can be found on You Tube.

For recording what is happening on a computer display, Cam Studio is a free and open source program for Windows. Cam studio can be downloaded from http://camstudio.org. Cam Studio is great for making video tutorials such as those that demonstrate how to use computer programs. On some machines with decent speeds, it may be able to record streaming movies. The program is very simple to use as well. For Linux users, Recordmydesktop is recommended. Recordmydesktop can be downloaded at http://sourceforge.net/projects/recordmydesktop/ or it can be installed using one's distribution specific package manager.

For musicians, software, and video content producers, CD, DVD, and Blue Ray publish on demand websites are listed below:

http://www.acutrack.com

http://www.cd-fulfillment.com

http://www.createspace.com

http://www.customcd.com

http://www.deltalprinting.com

On-line Content

On-line content refers to anything that is published on the Internet. Documents, videos and audio files are discussed earlier in this chapter. This particular part focuses on building and publishing web sites. From the end user perspective, publishing a website involves four different aspects. These are setting up a domain name, setting up domain name service (DNS), finding a provider to host the site, and adding content.

Many providers provide only some of these services, some providers provide all of these services. Each of these aspects and various pitfalls are discussed in this chapter.

Domain names are the names of websites such as google.com, yahoo.com, bit.ly, etc. In order to set up a domain name, one has to sign up through a company called a domain registrar. Commonly used domain registrars include http://www.register.com, http://www.godaddy.com, http://www.1and1.com, etc. Fees for registering a domain can vary from a few dollars to tens of thousands of dollars depending if the domain was previously registered. There is also a recurring annual or multi-annual fee in order to keep the domain once it is registered. One place that offers a quick comparison shopping guide is http://www.regselect.com/.

A person wishing to register a domain

should make a list of the domains he or she wants as well as a list of alternate domains should the most desired domain name be taken. After this is done, a person should visit several different registrars' websites in order to compare prices and services offered. However, a person should NOT yet search to see if a desired domain name is taken until he or she is ready to make an immediate purchase. This is due to the fact that some unscrupulous registrars, domain search services or hosting sites will actually buy up often searched for domain names in the hopes of reselling the searched for names at a higher price. The practice of doing this is known as domain squatting. If a person hires another to handle building the website, the person should register the domain him or herself to avoid having the hired person stealing the domain should their be any type of disagreement. Registering a domain name is not hard and can be done by just about anyone who has a valid credit card number and funds available. Once a person has decided upon a domain name a few alternatives, and on the registrar to be used he or she should immediately attempt to register the domain. Once this is done, the person owns the domain until he or she lets it lapse. Another pitfall to avoid is using the same company for the registrar and web hosting service. This is due to the fact that if there is any disagreement, the web hosting company will be able to hold the domain name hostage as well as the content.

Once a domain has been registered, the person registering the domain will be asked for the domain name or IP address of the name servers he or she wants to use. This can be entered at the time of domain registration or any time thereafter.

A name server converts the domain name to an IP address. It acts much like the telephone 411 service or even the phone book. In most cases, a company that sells web hosting services also offers the use of their domain name service as well. In fact, most even automatically include this service in their price. It is safe to use the same company to provide both DNS and web hosting because if a person changes service, all he or she has to do is log into their account with the domain registrar and point the name server address to their new provider. Most providers will give instructions on how to do this.

After a domain is registered, the content that the domain owner wants web surfers to see must be stored somewhere in order to be accessed. This somewhere is called, a web hosting service. Web hosting services vary so much in the feature that they have. Depending upon the expertise of the person who is setting up the website, there are several factor to take into account. One of these include web design templates. Some web hosting services, such as offered at http://www.godaddy.com, offer a step by step design template that allow users to select graphic files from their computers to post on their new website as well as allowing them to enter (or paste) text to the website. Other web hosting services allow users to upload the content that they have created themselves to the host. One place that allows people to compare web hosting services is http://webhostinggeeks.com. Another is http://www.tophosts.com.   As stated before, a user can upload his or her own content created entirely on his or her computer, or he or she can use any site building template offered by the web host provider. In cases where the user decides to use content on own computer, he or she must use some method of getting the content to the web hosting provider. Some web hosting providers provide this functionality by using a web portal that is accessible via a regular web browser such as Mozilla Firefox, Google Chrome, or even Internet explorer. Other use something called ftp also known as File Transfer Protocol. Just about every modern operating system on the market includes an FTP program to allow this type of upload, but there are also free graphical programs that are much easier to operate available for free download. One such program is called, "Filezilla." It is an open source program available for a free download by visiting, http://filezilla-project.org. Another is available as a Mozilla Firefox plugin. It is called FireFTP and is available by visiting http://fireftp.mozdev.org. These are the ones used by the author.

If one wants to change hosting providers, he or she should obtain a new hosting provider before canceling the old. The new hosting provider, if providing DNS service too, will need to provide the user with name server information. The person purchasing the new hosting service needs to upload his or her content to the new provider. After that, the person who changed to the new hosting service will need to log into the registrar's website and change the name server information for the domain registered. This type of transitioning is required because it does take some time for name servers all over the Internet to become updated with the new information. Sometimes this time required is only a few hours, and other times, it may take days.

Software

Software is one of the prime examples of content that can be published on-line. There are several models of software distribution. These include Freeware, Free and Open Source (FOSS), Shareware, Advertisement supported, and purchasable. Software developers can release their software under one or more of the listed publication models depending upon motivations of the developer.

Freeware is any software that is available for no cost to the user.

With freeware, there is no cost to the user for utilizing the software, but there may be restrictions on where such software can be obtained. The person or company releasing such freeware may allow others to distribute the software at no cost or may charge others for the privilege of distributing the software when it is bundled with other software (or hardware). Freeware may also be restricted to personal, non-commercial use. Freeware is generally closed source, and derivative works may not be created from it. Examples of freeware include QuickFix, Combofix, MalwareBytes Antimalware, E-Sword, Flash Player, Adobe Reader, and Ccleaner. For the developer of freeware, the freeware may serve as advertising for the person or company producing the software. People who use freeware products may be enticed to purchase paid software produced by the same person or company. Another reason to release software on the freeware model is for charitable or altruistic reasons. The developer of E-sword, for example, has released that software for the purpose of spreading the Gospel. Freeware can be published to http://www.download.com via http://www.upload.com, http://www.filehippo.com, as well as many other sites.

Free and Open Source Software (FOSS) is software that is considered totally free or almost totally free. An important distinction between FOSS and freeware is the fact that there are few restrictions on re-distribution of FOSS software and that derivative works may generally be created based upon the FOSS software. It also means that the source code for such software is available to the user for modification and redistribution. Restrictions or licensing requirements of such software is generally used to protect freedom rather than restricting it. Under one such licensing scheme, the GNU Public License (GPL), such software may be redistributed and derivative works created from it only as long as the person who creates such derivative works also releases the source code of the derivative work. With such software, one may even charge money for the redistribution of FOSS software. Linux, Apache, GIMP, Asterisk, Firefox, Chromium, Asterisk are just a very few number of software product that are released under the FOSS model. Open source software can be published through http://www.sourceforge.net, http://www.freshmeat.net as well as sites allowing the distribution of freeware, advertisement supported software, and freeware.

Shareware is software based on the try before buy business model. Some shareware products remain fully functioning for a limited time or number of uses. Other shareware products include limited features with the rest being available once the user purchases the software. In many cases, users of shareware can be enticed to buy such software in order to either keep using the software after its trial period expires or in other to get to use all the features of the software. In order to get access to the full version or to continue use of the software, a user may have to either re-download the purchased version or be required to enter a serial number which is supplied upon purchase. Examples of shareware include mIRC, Registry Mechanic, GIF Construction Set as well as many others. Shareware can be published to http://www.download.com via http://www.upload.com, http://www.filehippo.com, and many other sites.

The advertisement supported software business model operates by letting advertisers pay for the software instead of the user. The program will either display advertisements in the program's execution window, cause an advertisement window to pop up. More insidious programs will allow advertising companies to install additional software on the user's computer. It is the opinion of the author that the only ethical advertising supported programs are those that display an advertising window within the program itself where the user can click on the advertisement in order to be sent to the sponsor's website. Any software that changes a browser's home page or installs programs that displays pop up advertisements elsewhere on the user's computer will bring negative attention to the product advertised. Unfortunately, many advertisement supported programs do just that, and the author considers them malicious software.

Some promoted software is only available in exchange for money. Examples of such software is Microsoft Office, Microsoft Windows, Vegas, as well as many others. Software developers selling software in this manner usually have a website available where such software can be order or sometimes even downloaded after payment is made. Software sold in this manner should be promoted in much the same way as a video, music album, or book.

Free Advertising

Much talent and many good products are simply overlooked or are never heard of simply because it is so hard for the producers of such products to be seen or heard over the din of advertising put out by big companies. Fortunately, due to the Internet and publishing on demand, there are many new ways for people to get heard and sell their products. Social networking allows people to get their work published or their physical products promoted.

MySpace, which is a popular social network, offers free accounts to personal users, musicians, comedians, and film makers. For content producers, choosing the appropriate account profile is essential to getting the most out of promoting through Myspace. Myspace allows musicians to create a profile page and fit their music into many different categories. It also allows musicians to upload music tracks to their profile so that potential audiences can listen to what they produce. My Space is located at

http://www.myspace.com.

There are other sites for promoting music and some of them are http://www.emusic.com

http://www.youtube.com
(Works even better with music videos or a video of a gig).

The most popular social networking site at the time of this book is written is
http://www.facebook.com.

Facebook allows its users to post updates as to what they are doing as well as links to website they like. When people connect with friends or strangers, for that matter, whatever they post on their profile is need by people with whom they are "friends." This provides ample opportunity to post a link to a product's website.

Another way to generate free advertisement is by creating a blog. A blog is a personal web page or website where a person can express his or her opinion, recommend certain products, or give instructions on how to accomplish a task. Other ways of promoting products include posting how to information on other people's blogs or forums, and writing articles for on-line newspapers.

Http://www.blogspot.com is one

website where people can set up a blog for free. Other very popular places where people can set up a free blog include http://www.blogger.com, http://www.wordpress.com, and http://www.livejournal.com.

Blogs related to specific fields of interests are also available. For example, if someone is promoting a book related to breeding dogs, he or she can search the Internet for *dog blogs.* Specialty blog sites may allow users to set up their own blogs, or they may allow users to post comments and their own articles to the blog. In either case, an informative article with a link to the user's website is a good promotion technique.

A forum is much like a blog. Forums are discussions posted to websites and are usually in a question and answer (or comment) format. Many sites specializing in topics offer free access to forums. For someone promoting a video game paying handbook can search the Internet for *game forums*.

When posting to blogs or forums, one should provide information relevant to the topic being discussed. One can mention his or her product as a byline and include a link to their web site. It is a good idea to read the blog or forum rules to see what is allowed and what is specifically forbidden. A few forums and blog prohibit links to commercial websites. The more links leading to a website, blog or product, the higher will rank on search engines it will be.

Chapter 6 - Virtualization and Emulation

A virtualization program is an application that imitates an actual computer, smartphone, game console, or other hardware. Virtualization is the process of running one operating system inside a program running under another operating system. A virtualization program looks like just another program to the operating system that the computer boots into. A common scenario in which this is used is when a computer running Microsoft Windows has an icon on the desktop that allows the user to open the virtualization program in order to run, for example, Linux. A good use of a virtualization program is to allow a user to enjoy the advantages of different operating systems at the same time. It is a way of saving time and money by not having to buy and run (energy costs) extra computers. It is also a way to save money by not having to buy video game consoles.

For example, one can take advantage of the easy set up, administration, and compatibility with proprietary programs offered by Microsoft Windows operating system while at the same time enjoying Linux's ability to use the Internet without having to worry too much about a malicious software infection taking over the computer.

The author uses virtualization to run Microsoft Windows on his Linux laptop. The author uses Windows when testing proprietary programs available only for Windows. He also uses Windows for tasks that needs to be done quickly if using Linux for the same task would require a longer time to get set up. The author will then take the time later on to set up Linux to perform the same task.

Virtualization also allows a computer user to try out or become familiar with operating systems he or she may need or want to learn. It is another way to try new things. Virtualization also offers the advantage of isolating the bad effects of a rogue or malfunctioning program or operating system. The operating system which is installed on the computer and into which the computer boots when turned on is called the host operating system. The operating system which is run in the virtualization program's window is called the guest operating system. Two very popular virtualization program discussed in this book are Virtual Box and Vmware

Player. There are also quite a few others, but for the sake of brevity, these will be the ones discussed. Virtualization and emulation programs that imitate gaming consoles are also discussed.

Virtual Box

One virtualization application that is popular is the the Virtualbox program that can be downloaded from http://www.virtualbox.org. The Virtualbox application even emulates hardware circuitry such as sound cards, graphics cards and network devices. Oracle offers the Virtualbox program under several different licenses. These include the GPL, PUEL, and a paid license. The version listed under the PUEL (Personal Use and Evaluation) license offers the best combination of features and ease of use for most home users (as well as some limited business use). A technician installing Virtualbox on multiple computers in a business setting will likely use the paid license. The GPL version is of very limited use an does not include many of the ease of use and setup feature available under the other licenses.

Since Virtualbox is a program that imitates a computer, it allows the user to set the features and capabilities that are presented to the guest operating system. Virtualbox allows the user to set the amount of RAM that is available to the guest operating system. It also allows the user to set the amount of hard drive space that is available to the guest operating system as well.

Both of these cannot be set to any amount that exceeds (or meets) the amount of memory or hard drive space available to the host operating system. With Virtualbox, a file that is used to emulate the hard drive to the guest operating system can be set to a maximum size, and an option to allow this file to grow in size as more programs and data are added to the guest operating system can be set.

When setting up a new guest operating system on Virtualbox, a user will have to do the following (in order):

Click on the "New" button. The user will be presented with a new window asking for VM Name and OS Type. The user will need to enter a name for the virtual machine (whatever is desired). The user will then need to click on the drop down menu to select which type of operating system to install.   Choices include Microsoft Windows, Linux, Solaris, BSD, IBM

OS/2, Mac OSX, and others. On some versions of virtual box, there will be a drop down box under the OS Type Drop down box prompting the user to select version of operating system (Win9x, XP, Linux distribution, etc). Once this is complete, the user will need to click the "Next" button.

The next screen that show up will ask for the amount of ram to devote to the guest operating system. This should at most be half of the total memory (RAM) available on the computer on which Virtualbox is installed.

After that, the user will be asked to select the size of the virtual hard drive space available to the guest operating system.

Virtualbox allows the guest operating system to use devices such as those that provide sound, networking, etc. through virtual or imitation hardware. This means that for example, the host may have an Intel based sound hardware, but the guest operating system, will see this card as whatever is configured in the Virtualbox settings.

The sound cards that are imitated by Virtualbox are Soundblaster 16 and the Realtek ICH AC97. The guest operating system must provide the driver software for the imitated hardware. If the guest operating system is Windows Vista or Windows 7, then Virtualbox should be configured to use the Realek ICH AC97. For the guest operating system, the Soundblaster 16 drivers can be downloaded from http://www.creative.com. The ICH AC97 driver can be downloaded from http://www.realtek.com.

Virtualbox also presents an imitation network card to the guest operating system. Virtualbox offers a choice of several network cards to be supported by the guest operating system. Again, the network card that is actually used by the computer running the host operating system does not matter as long as it is properly set up and is in a usable state. The choices offered to the guest operating system include PCnet-PCI II (Am79C970A), PCnet-FAST III (Am79C973), Intel PRO 1000 MT Desktop (82540EM), Intel PRO 1000 T Server (82543GC), and Intel PRO 1000 MT Server (82545EM).

The guest operating system will sometimes include drivers for one of these network cards in its standard installation. For virtual card for which drivers are not included, one will have to obtain them from the manufacturer's website.

Another consideration when it comes to networking a guest operating system is the type of network connection desired. The type of network connection is referred to in the VirtualBox manual as a, "Networking mode." The five Networking modes available with VirtualBox are listed below:

Not attached – This mode makes the guest operating system act as if there is a network card attached, but that it is not connected to any network.

NAT – This mode allows Internet access for web browsers, email clients, and other client software in the guest operating system but prevents other computers from being able to access services such as email servers, web hosting, etc. from outside of the guest operating system.

Bridged Adapter – This mode allows the guest operating system to appear as if it is a separate computer on the same network as the host operating system. It will allow the guest operating system to have its own IP address and allow the guest to host services that are available to computers on the same network as the host operating system.

Internal Network – This allows the guest operating system to form a network with the host and any other guest operating system currently running on the same host. A virtual network card is also created on the host in order to provide the networking between currently running guest and host operating systems. In other words, it is a network separate from any external network to which the host is connected.

Host-only Adapter – This is used to create a network containing the host and currently running guest operating systems without using the host's network interface.

USB devices also work with Virtualbox. Rather than appearing as a different device to the guest operating system, USB devices installed on the host computer are directly available to the guest operating system. To use a USB device within the guest operating system requires the device drivers to be installed on the guest operating system. It will be accessible as if the guest operating system is the host.

With the thousands of different USB

devices available, it is impossible to list them all in this book. However, if there is a driver available for the device in a version that works on the guest operating system, then the device should work.

When configuring device settings for the Virtualbox program, one should be aware that with the exception of USB devices, the settings of the Virtualbox are not changeable unless the guest operating system is powered down.

Virtualbox is not the only program out there that can emulate and entire computer, but it is one of the best, and it is capable of being downloaded for free. It also has a very liberal license for a commercial software package. It also comes with no time limit on its functionality.

Vmware Player

Another virtual machine program is Vmware Player which is available from http://www.vmware.com/products/player. Unfortunately, licensing restrictions require that the free version only be used for personal, noncommercial use. It also requires free registration in which the user's name, email address, city, zip code, and country is required. The download site lists VM Player being available for only Microsoft Windows and Linux. Because of the more restrictive licensing and requirement for personal information in order to download, this software is not discussed any further.

Other virtualization programs are listed on-line. Some of them are commercial, and others are open source. One list of virtualization programs can be found at http://www.ask.com/wiki/Comparison_of_platform_virtual_machines. This site is user supported, and changes made be made by users. More virtualization programs can be found by searching for *virtualization programs*.

Gaming Console Emulators

Gaming console emulators are programs that allow games created for game consoles to run on a desktop or laptop computer. Game console emulators offer several advantages to the computer user. These advantage include low or no cost games, the ability to play home brew games, the ability to play copied games, and the fact that the gaming console is not required in order to play these games.

There are also two main disadvantages to using a console emulation program. These are the fact that users in many cases, cannot use the controls that are purchased for or come with the game console and the game being played may be slower, have less screen resolution, and may sometimes be quirky when running under emulation. Even though there are disadvantages, many people use game console emulation with very few problems.

When there are problems, users can check to see if there are updates or newer versions of the game emulation software.

A list of game emulators can be found at http://www.emulator-zone.com/. Some of these programs require an additional download in order to work. In many cases, this additional download is a copy of the console's B.I.O.S. The B.I.O.S. Is the program that tells the console how to start up and load games. Because the B.I.O.S. Is copyrighted software, it is not included in the emulation software. Check with laws applicable in your jurisdiction to determine if downloading the B.I.O.S. Is legal. To find the B.I.O.S. Image file, all one has to do is search on-line. An example of search terms for the PlayStation B.I.O.S. would be, *"PlayStation BIOS."*

A few free game emulators are listed below and on the next pages:

Microsoft

Cxbx emulates X-box. It can be downloaded from http://www.caustik.com/cxbx.

Nintendo

Project64 emulates Nintendo 64. It can be downloaded from http://www.pj64-emu.com.

DS NocashGBA (No$GBA) emulates DS. It can be downloaded from http://www.nogba.com.

Visual Boy Advance emulates Game Boy and Game Boy Advanced. It can be downloaded from http://vba.ngemu.com/

BGB also emulates Game Boy and can be downloaded from http://bgb.bircd.org.

Gamecube Dolphin emulates Gamecube and can be downloaded from http://www.dolphin-emulator.com.

NES FCEUX emulates the NES and can be downloaded from http://fceux.com/web/home.html

Super Nintendo ZSNES emulates Super Nintendo. It can be downloaded from http://www.zsnes.com.

Wii Dolphin emulates Wii and can be downloaded from http://www.dolphin-emulator.com.

Sega

Sega has emulators for several of its consoles. Some of these programs require additional downloads which are explained on the program's website.

Dreamcast Chankast emulates the

Dreamcast on X86-64 bit computers running Windows It can be downloaded at http://www.chanka.org.
Null also emulates Dreamcast. It can be downloaded from http://www.emulator-zone.com/doc.php/dreamcast/nulldc.html or http://code.google.com/p/nulldc/

Kega Fusion emulates Game Gear, Genesis, and Master System. It can be downloaded from http://www.eidolons-inn.net/tiki-index.php?page=Kega.

Gens is another program that emulates Genesis. It can be downloaded from http://www.segaretro.org/Gens.

Satourne emulates Saturn

http://satourne.consollection.com

This one can be difficult to set up, so visitation to http://www.emu-forum.com/index.php?showtopic=501 is recommended. For this system, one needs to obtain an image file of the B.I.O.S. for the gaming system.

Sony

EPSXe emulates the Playstation. It can be downloaded from http://www.epsxe.com. One also needs to obtain a B.I.O.S. Image for this game.

PCSX2 emulates Playstation 2. It can be downloaded at http://pcsx2.net. One also needs to obtain a B.I.O.S. Image for this game.

PCSP emulates Playstation Portable.

It can be downloaded from
http://www.pcsp-emu.com.

Some of these emulators work well
with most games. Some are hit and
miss, and some work only with a few
games. The hackers who write
emulators usually have no guide to go
by and must painstakenly reverse
engineer each console for which their
program works. This involves lots of
research, testing, programming, etc.
If something doesn't work entirely,
don't blame the hacker. He or she is
working only with the information that
he or she can obtain.

Chapter 7 -
The Wonderful World of
Free Unix

What is Unix? Unix is an operating system dating back to the early 1970's. Those were the days when computers were large and served multiple users. Unix was built from the ground up to provide users protection from each other. This protection was meant to prevent users from accidentally or maliciously erasing or altering each others files or work. Unix is very significant today simply because it has been modified and its features extended to keep up with the times.

Today, there are many different branches or offshoots of Unix. Because of its long history and its initial dedication to security, Unix has remained a strong competitor to the various Microsoft operating systems that are popular today.

Most desktop computers today run operating systems made by Microsoft. This is due to the fact that Microsoft had focused upon ease of use rather than security. Microsoft's operating systems were first intended to run on home computers that were used to balance checkbooks, play games, etc. Until computers were connected to each other via networks such as the Internet, this was perfectly fine. As computers became more connected, criminals have taken advantage of the weakness of Microsoft product security to create mischief. As a result, Microsoft has been in a game of catch up in order to protect its users (and to keep users coming back to buy more). Unix, on the other hand, has had to be adapted to be more user friendly.

Even though most people believe that they use Microsoft Windows only, they are mistaken. Unix is found on many, many computers that are used to process email, serve web pages, convert domain names such as www.linux.com to their IP address, and to route Internet traffic. Just about everyone who has used the Internet is in fact an indirect user of Unix. Unix and a Unix clone called Linux are making a resurgence among desktop users as well.

Apple's operating system is based upon a version of Unix called BSD. According to one source, Unix and Linux make up about nine percent of the desktop operating system market.

<u>Linux</u>

Linux is an Unix clone. The core part of Linux, the kernel, was originally written by an engineering student named Linus Torvalds. Linus wanted an affordable version of Unix to run on his computer but could not find one already on the market. Necessity is the mother of invention, and Linus began work on the Linux Kernel. Other people such as Richard Stallman had also started a project with the goal of creating a free Unix like operating system.

Linus's kernel and Richard's programs were eventually merged into a work that became freely redistributable. The resulting operating system was distributed under a very liberal license that allowed people to sell it, modify it, or give it away for free with only one condition – the source code (the language in which the programs are written by a human) for the modification would have to be made available upon request. What this has done is allow people to build upon the work of others without fear of reprisal. Linux has moved from being a clunky operating system that only ran on a 386 computer to a full featured operating system that runs many different type of hardware. Linux can be found on telephones, cellphones, routers, digital video recorders, televisions, alarms, video games, PDA's and even some wrist watches. Linux runs on the following processors: x86, x86-64, Alpha, Blackfin, ARM, Amtel, Axis Motorola's 68k, Fujitsu, PA-RISK, H8, Itanium, SGI, M32R, Microblaze, MIPS, PowerPC, SPARC, SuperH, S+core, Tilera, Xtensa, as well as others. In other words, it runs on many types of hardware that many have never even heard of.

As Linux grows, so does the number of contributors. Linux is used and supported by many different companies and hardware vendors. Since there are so many different devices on which Linux runs and since people can freely write derivative works, Linux is now available in many versions also called distributions. One of the biggest advantages of Linux is the fact that it will run on most any capable hardware, it is relatively secure, and best of all, it is free.

Programs that are licensed with the same type of license that Linux has are in many cases as good as or even better than their closed source counterparts. In fact, this book has been completely written and designed on a Linux based computer. Linux is the author's favorite operating system. Linux is also relatively immune to malware such as worms, viruses, trojans, etc. This is due not only to the fact that Linux is based upon an operating system (Unix) that was built with security in mind but also due to the mentality of its developers. Most programs for Linux are what is called, "open source." Open source means that the human readable source code used to make programs for Linux is available for anyone to examine and modify. Rather than depending on a few hundred or even thousands of paid developers to make desired changes, Linux and like projects have an entire army of paid and unpaid developers who are able to make positive changes in accordance to the knowledge and skills they have.

Comparing Linux to cars, means that the users not only are able to operate the car, but they are also able to look under the hood and tinker with the engine, transmission, and other parts. Using the same analogy with Microsoft and other operating systems with little or no public source code disclosure, users get a car with the engine compartment welded shut. They are able to drive the car, but will have a difficult time in getting to innards in order to tinker.

The mentality of Linux and open source development is mostly based upon cooperation. Many develop and improve programs for their own use and then distribute or submit the improvements to main project developers. A large percentage of people who develop code for Microsoft based systems keep the source code for their products a closely guarded secret. For the most part, such secrecy is not tolerated among Linux users, and developers who practice such secrecy in many cases find themselves with a very small user base. Because of this fact, it becomes more difficult for malicious developers to sneak trojans, worms, and other malicious software to users. Any program, with sufficient privileges can steal data, erase files, be used to send spam, or take other malicious actions. This is just as true on Linux as it is on Microsoft based operating systems. Most companies or individuals who create versions or distributions of Linux compile Linux programs from source themselves. They do this because in many cases, they may make modifications so that the program will work better with other programs within the distribution. This means that there is greater chance that malicious developers will be exposed.

Because of the free nature of Linux, there are free programs that will perform most if not all or more task than equivalent programs costing hundreds if not thousand of dollars. A prime example of such a program is the Asterisk telephony software. Most commercial programs doing all the same things using Microsoft based operating systems will cost thousands of dollars.

With all of the advantages to using Linux, there are several factors that are preventing it from being the dominate desktop operating system. Each distribution has its own software installation or package management system. This make it more difficult to support people who use a different distribution of Linux. In addition, people generally dislike change. Even though Linux can be set up to act much like Microsoft based operating systems, it is not Windows. In addition, support for various peripherals or add on hardware is generally provided by developers for each distribution. While some support may be given by makers of hardware or peripherals, it is up to the distribution developers to make it work with their version of Linux. This is due to the fact that peripheral manufacturers are usually profit driven, and taking the time to customize software for each version of Linux costs money.

Those who want to try Linux and see if it meets their needs can do so by simply downloading a distribution and burning it to a CD or DVD. There are several distributions recommended by the author for beginners. These include Mandriva Linux which is available   at http://www.mandriva.com/en, Ubuntu Linux is available at http://www.ubuntu.com/,

OpenSuSE Linux available at http://www.opensuse.org/en/, and Fedora Linux available at http://fedoraproject.org/.

One should take to time to research each distribution to determine which one is best meets the need. There are also many other distributions with each catering to a specific need or desire.

Some of the distributions listed above have the option to run live from the CD in order to give a user the chance of testing without actually installing or wiping out their current operating system. Other ways of installing Linux along with Windows include dual booting. Dual booting allows a user to decide between starting Windows or Linux when the computer is first turned on. Another option is to run Linux at the same time Windows is running by using virtualization. Virtualization is discussed in some detail in chapter six of this book.

FreeBSD

FreeBSD is another clone of Unix. It was based upon Berkley Software Development Unix which in turn was based upon AT&T Unix. For legal reasons, it is not officially called, "Unix," but it is considered to be Unix compliant. FreeBSD is a complete operating system package including the kernel with device drivers and user utilities. FreeBSD is considered extremely stable and reliable.

FreeBSD development started around two years later later than Linux. Since the team that develops FreeBSD not only works on the kernel but also on the user programs as well, it has managed for the most part to keep FreeBSD uniform. In other words, there are not as many versions or distributions of FreeBSD. What this means is that experience with FreeBSD is not distribution specific. With Linux, on the other hand, each version or distribution has its own software package manager for installing, removing, and keeping records of the computer's software inventory.

This uniformity in BSD is an advantage for FreeBSD administrators. On the other hand, it also means that FreeBSD is available on in fewer hardware platforms than is Linux.

Currently, FreeBSD only supports x86 and x86-64 (Intel and AMD based) processors, PC98 processors, Powerpc processors, and sparc64 processors. It is available for download at http://www.freebsd.org.　　Many Linux binaries will run natively on FreeBSD.　In fact, since both Linux and FreeBSD are both open source products, just about all products available for one is also available for the other.

FreeBSD is an excellent operating system, but due to the fact that it has a relatively small user base, it is not as well known as its other free counterpart, Linux.　This means that Linux works with more types of hardware and peripherals.　FreeBSD will also run under a virtual machine such as VirtualBox.　As far as free Unix operating systems go, FreeBSD and Linux are the top contenders.

Open Solaris

A relatively minor player in the word of free Unix is an operating system called, Open Solaris. Open solaris can be downloaded from http://www.opensolaris.org.

Open Solaris was put out by Sun Microsystems in order to build the user and developer base for its proprietary operating system. When Sun was bought out by Oracle, the development of Open Solaris was discontinued. At the time this is written, another group started Illumos, a group dedicated to the continuing development of Open Solaris. Illumos has a website at URL http://www.illumos.org.

Hopefully, this project will continue to develop into a third robust clone of the Unix operating system. Open Solaris will run under the VirtualBox virtualization program. With its limited number of device drivers, it is not recommended that Open Solaris be run on end user desktop computers that use cameras, web cameras, printers, PDA'S, etc. Open Solaris has potential and is a decent operating to use for web, email, and DNS hosting.

As malicious software, stability, speed, and pricing issues continue to plague many Microsoft Windows users, free clones of Unix may become attractive to some of these users. For Microsoft loyalists, free Unix also offers an indirect benefit. Free Unix is a driver that will keep Microsoft innovating and improving their products in order to maintain its dominate market share.

Chapter 8 - Internet Connectivity

Many people take their broadband Internet connection for granted. There are those who only wish they could get a decent Internet connection. Many broadband deprived people live in either rural areas or areas where the local utilities for one reason or another simply refuse to provide service. In other places, the local monopoly simply charges too much for broadband to be affordable. Still, others may be traveling and be outside their service area.

Some area ISP's also filter, block, manage, throttle, or censor certain types of Internet traffic. This is called traffic shaping and is a bone of contention between Internet service providers, some of their customers, and the government. For those without broadband or who are subject to traffic shaping by their Internet provider do have other options for getting on-line.

One option is a cellular network card, these are available through many contract and prepaid cellular service providers. One company Virgin Mobile sells a WIFI hot spot that allows up to 5 different devices to connect to the Internet via Sprint's 3G network. The device also allows video streaming. The only disadvantage is that the connection may slow at times depending upon network congestion. It is possible to allow even more devices to use the MIFI device by setting up another wireless router as a wireless bridge and having the additional computers connect through the bridge rather than connecting directly through the MIFI device.

http://www.ezlan.net/router_AP.h
tml is a web page that provides instruction on how to do this.

Scanning for Open Networks

Another option is to use available open networks such as hot spots in McDonalds, coffee shops, book stores, and any other place where free access is provided. Important files can be uploaded or downloaded while visiting such establishments. However, beware of typing in any username or password to access websites unless the web URL starts with https://. Access to email server should also be done over an encrypted (SSL or TLS) connection. Information on how to set up encrypted email access can be obtain from the technical support staff or website of the email provider.

To scan for available networks, one needs to right click on the wireless network icon at the lower right hand side of the screen (near the time and date display in the task bar) and choose "view available networks." If the resulting window gives a message, "Windows cannot configure this wireless connection," then the user has another (vendor provided) program that manages the wireless network connection. The user can either use the vendor provided program to view network connections or try starting the Wireless Zero Configuration (WZC) service. Instructions for doing this can be found at http://support.microsoft.com/kb/871122

Once the window is opened, one selects the appropriate network and connects.

Convert Router into Wireless Bridge

Wireless routers are plugged into a wired Internet connection and allow a number of computers with wireless capabilities to connect to the wired Internet connection. A wireless bridge does just the opposite. A wireless bridge connects to to the Internet via the wireless connection and allows wired Ethernet connections from several computers that are plugged into the wireless bridge. This is good for computers that only have wired Ethernet capabilities. The author uses such a device for working on older model computers brought in for troubleshooting. The bridge is located on the work bench, and computers are connected to the bridge via Ethernet cables. Another use for a wireless bridge is for video game consoles that only provide for wired Ethernet connections. Another wireless router can actually be plugged into the bridge and be used to bypass limits imposed on the number simultaneous wireless connections that may be imposed upon a local wireless network.

The bridge makes a connection to the wireless router over the airwaves. Such bridges are expensive, and some can run into the hundreds of dollars. The good news is that many wireless routers can be converted into wireless bridges. In many cases, all it takes is the download and installation of software onto the wireless router. The specific how to for doing this depends upon the make and model of the router, and with so many different brands of routers out there, it would take hundreds of pages to discuss how to do this with each. Links will be provided to websites that have instructions on conversion for many commonly available routers. These are listed below:

Linksys WRT54G:
http://www.dvrplayground.com/article/12254/Converting-a-Linksys-WRT54G-GS-Into-An-Ethernet-Bridge/

Other routers:
http://www.dd-wrt.com/wiki/index.php/Supported_Devices
(There is an underscore (_) character between Supported and Devices).

There is another way to connect video games or other devices with only wired Ethernet interfaces to a wireless router, and it involves having a computer with both wired and wireless capability nearby. The gaming console is plugged into the wired connection, and the computer is connected to the Internet via its wireless network connection. Internet connection sharing is used to share the computer's connection with the gaming console (or any other device). The step by step instruction on how to do this can be found at http://support.microsoft.com/kb/306126 for XP, and http://windows.microsoft.com/en-US/windows-vista/Using-ICS-Internet-Connection-Sharing   For Windows Vista/7.

What People Need to Know about Their Internet Provider

In the constant quest for money, some Internet service providers charge an additional fee to allow more than one computer to be connected to an Internet account. This is common with cable companies.

When a subscriber first signs up with an Internet provider that charges such networking a fee, it is common for the software on the setup disk to record the hardware (also known as a MAC) address of the network card that is connected to the supplied modem and use this address to cause the modem to allow connection to the Internet from a computer with this hardware address.   If a person connects another computer to a cable modem, and the Internet is no longer reachable, then blockage due to an unauthorized network interface should be suspected.

Spoofing Hardware Addresses

Fortunately, most routers and access points have a feature that allows this hardware address to be cloned or spoofed.   When a router or access point is set up to spoof a computer's hardware address and is connected to a modem, the modem sees the router as the computer on which the account was set up.

The user should download the user manual for his or her router before any attempt is made at spoofing the physical address. The user can search on-line using the router's model number and the words *"User Manual."* *W*ith so many models of routers out there, it would take about 40 pages to describe most of them. However, this information should be easy for a user to obtain.

In order to spoof the hardware address of the computer that is registered to the cable modem, the address must be first obtained. This address can be obtained by pressing the Windows key (The one with the Windows logo on it) and *R* at the same time, clearing out whatever is in the box and typing in *cmd.* After that, the user needs to press the enter or return key and when the black window appears, the user then type in *ipconfig /all* and press the enter key again. There will be a list of cards and under each will be a label, "Physical Address." The user will have to locate the card which has IP addresses listed for the Default Gateway, DHCP Server, and DNS Servers. These addresses will be in a form similar to 192.168.1.1, 10.22.11.1, or any other value. The user may have to scroll up or down to locate the card with these values, but once it is found, he or she can then copy the physical address.

The physical address will look something like 00-07-E9-6F-37-21 (the actual numbers and letters will be different). Once this number is obtained, the user can then unplug from the cable modem and plug the computer into his or her router. The router should not be plugged into the modem yet.

The user can then use the instruction manual for the router to log into it and change the router's MAC or physical address so that it matches the copied Physical address from the network card.

Avoiding Throttling and Site Blocking

Many workplace networks, public WIFI hot spots, and other networks block websites and content deemed by the operators to be objectionable. In many cases, the software that is used to block content also blocks harmless content as well.

If a user wants access to information

that is contained within a blocked website, there are options for getting that information.

Google, for example maintains a cache or local copy of many different websites. Users can access this cache by simply using a keyword, "cache:" then the URL of the page to be accessed. For example, if www.congregationyhwhpc.com is blocked by the network administrator, it may very well be accessible by visiting Google and typing "cache:www.congregationyhwhpc.com" in the search box. Another way of accessing a blocked page is by visiting http://www.archive.org and typing in the address of the blocked website there and then clicking on the appropriate date.

Another website that lists available

proxy   servers   is
http://www.mywebproxies.com.
At this website, one will see a list of
web proxies. All one has to do is visit
one of the listed websites and then
type in the desired address into a
form and then retrieve the web page.
If all else fails, one can simply search
the Internet for web proxies and
sooner or later will find a website that
works.

Chapter 9
Privacy and Security

A majority of people pay very little attention to privacy and security issues other than locking doors or windows on their homes or cars. A few go a little bit further and install security system in their homes and cars and think they are safe. For the most part, they are as safe as many, but there are still vulnerabilities that they need to address to improve their security situation. Many of these same people will be the first to state, "I have nothing to hide." or "I don't have any secrets or any special information that needs to be protected." In both cases, they could not be more wrong. A social security number paired with the corresponding valid name and date of birth is valuable information for identity thieves. This information can be used by illegal aliens to obtain work. This in and of itself may not be bad depending upon one's view of illegal immigration, but this use of personal information can lead to harassment by government agencies such as the I.R.S. or law enforcement. This is especially true if the illegal alien happens to be a criminal.

Another use of the this personal information can be to open bank accounts and take out loans in the person's name. Identity theft is one of the fastest growing area of crime, and with a few simple steps, one can protect one's self. When it comes to information security, the same thing applies. People in many cases think, "I have nothing on my computer that anyone would want. This too cannot be further from the truth.

Friend's lists and contact information

is very valuable to spammers, those who spread malicious software. An insecure Internet connection can be used by people to download and store child pornography, pirated material or used as a proxy for illegal activity. When an official investigator detects an Internet connection being used in illegal activity, the first one to get the knock on their door is the person whose connection was taken over. If that person's computer is used to host illegal activity and the computer is searched, then the victim will have a very expensive lawyer bill and may very well spend time in prison. Just about all of this can be prevented by taking simple steps in maintaining security. Most people are blissfully unaware how easy it is for a prospective employer, family member, or even nosy neighbor to spy upon a person using their very own technology against them. This chapter discusses information on how to protect one's self against various intrusions.

Electronic Security

There are many different types of people or organizations that want to collect peoples' personal information. These include thieves intent on stealing money from bank or credit card accounts or who sell the personal information to spammers or other thieves, companies that send targeted advertisements to people, companies that study trends in peoples' likes or dislikes, or governmental agencies conducting investigations or spy campaigns on citizens.

Information may also be stolen by nosy friends, family member, or even personal enemies. Such information can be used in gossip, to obtain even more information, revenge, or even to embarrass a target.

Any of these can present a threat to individuals. Account thieves can steal identities, drain bank accounts, send spam via a user's email account, or even sell personal information to other thieves. Organizations that collect information for targeted advertisement campaigns can use personal information to entice a person to spend money that he or she may not originally intend to spend. In addition, such organizations may fail to adequately protect personal information and allow such information to be stolen by those who will use it to engage in electronic theft.

Organizations or businesses that study trends in consumer likes and dislikes sell or give this information to other companies which use such information to determine demand for certain products and services. This information can be used to decide whether to raise prices if demand indicates that raising prices would be profitable. It can also be used to decide whether to cancel a certain product's production. A government agency may use personal information in the conduct of legitimate investigations, political retribution, or to decide whether to place an individual on certain watch lists. In this day and age, one does not have to be doing anything wrong to be associated with wrongful activity.

Information can be pilfered from people in many different ways. One of the most common ways is to access a computer or other electronic device used by the targeted person. Any device that is connected to the traditional telephone service, a cellular network, a computer network, transmits a radio signal, or is left where it can be picked up unobserved is at risk for revealing information about its owner or user. Such devices include computers, answering machines, traditional telephones, cellular telephones, home entertainment devices, V.O.I.P. telephones, wireless (or wired) routers, home security devices, and one of the most insidious, the smart (cellular) phone. Another vulnerability in electronic security is the dependence upon Caller ID information that is displayed when there is an incoming call. Caller ID can be easily spoofed or faked by subscribing to one of many different Voice Over IP service providers.

Indicators of information security

breaches or surveillance take many forms. These include other people knowing information that is supposed to be private, unexplained credit card charges, collections agencies calling to collect on accounts not known to the victim, being only slightly outbid by competitors in business, etc.

There are several ways of detecting electronic eavesdropping and detecting whether private information is being disclosed by "loose lips" or actual surveillance. This chapter discusses ways of protecting personal information using common sense and free or inexpensive techniques to secure all kinds of electronic items against the theft and or disclosure of personal information. Much of this information deals with the setting of passwords, filtering connections, enabling encryption, and careful downloading and use of applications.

There are so many different brands of devices out there that it would take several volumes to give specific information on how to configure each and every one of them. However, in most cases, such information is available on-line free. This information can be found by typing in the model number of the device as well as the words, "*user manual*" or "*installation manual*." For example, to find the user manual for a Linksys WRT-54g router, one would type in the words, "*WRT-54g user manual*" (try the search with and without quotes) into any search engine. It may take a few minutes to locate the information since there are many sites that try to sell such information. Another option is to go to the manufacturers' web page and look up the information in the support section.

Pictures, recordings, and video files

can contain much embedded information that can cause trouble for a user. Many devices and programs that create files such as music, videos, documents, pictures, etc. may embed identifying information such as model and serial number, location information (for G.P.S. equipped devices), user names, author names, etc. This information is found in exif headers among other places. One cross platform, open source program that will show information that is embedded within files is called, "exiftools." This program and corresponding documentation can be downloaded from http://www.sno.phy.queensu.ca/~phil/exiftool/. One way to remove such information from a graphic or video file is to use a third party editor to convert or export the original file to either another format or to make a minor change and save the file.

Exiftools can then be run again on the saved file to ensure unwanted information is removed.

Smart Phones and PDA's

While most people tend to be cautious about what they do on a personal computer, man of these same people do not apply the same principle to the use of their smart phone. The smart phone contains a user's contacts list that include family, friends, and co-workers. It also has an embedded serial number that may uniquely identify the phone to various advertisement networks. The bad part is the fact that this number cannot be removed or changed without encountering great difficulty in doing so. This number may also be made available to applications that run on the phone. In fact, there are quite a few applications that transmit this number along with other personal information to companies that write the applications. Some of these companies sell this information to advertisers. Another thing that most smart phones can transmit is the physical location of the phone itself. This information, too, is available to applications that may transmit such information. Some phones will pop up a dialog asking for permission before location information is transmitted. On phones with this feature, the user should take note of which application is trying to obtain record information and choose carefully as to whether recording is allowed. On other phones, there is no permission dialog.

Smart phones or any phone running Symbian OS or Windows mobile operating system, Blackberries, iPhones, Android, as well as many others phones are vulnerable to having spy ware installed. This spy ware can be installed by anyone having physical access to a target phone. The phone is connected to a computer via a USB cable, and the software is loaded onto the phone, or it can be downloaded to the phone via an Internet connection. It can also be downloaded to the phone by using Blue Tooth in some cases. Once installed, the software can be hard to detect via software methods. A website selling phone spy ware, http://www.flexispy.com, shows some of the capabilities of such spy ware. Other software such as games and other applications may also embed code with spy ware capabilities. Government agencies can also sometimes install spy ware that works even when a phone is turned off. Some of the truly paranoid will remove the battery in their cell phone unless they are expecting a call or about to make one. Removing the battery is a sure fire way to prevent the cell phone from being used as a spy gadget.

On phones that use the Global System for Mobile Communications (GSM) protocol such as phone that use AT&T, T-Mobile, Cingular, and Tracfone service, there are some indicators that can be used to determine how much a phone transmits. One can place these phones near the speakers of a desktop computer system, and sounds can be heard through the speakers when these phones are transmitting voice and data. One should do this with the phone to familiarize one's self with the sounds emitted. This should be done when using the phone in conversation, text messaging, and Internet use. The phone should also be left near the computer speakers in order to see how often it intermittently transmits ping signals with the local cell phone tower. If the (computer) speakers are continuously making these sounds while not in use, this is an indicator of possible surveillance or spy activity.

On phones that use the Code Division Multiple Access (CDMA) communications protocol such as T-Mobile and Sprint, these sounds are nowhere near as audible. Other indicators of surreptitious transmission include unusually short periods of time between having to charge the phone and phones that remain warm even when not in use. When cell phones transmit, they consume much more battery power and therefore become warm.

One countermeasure that will protect a phone user is for the user to set his or her phone up to require an unlock code in order to use the phone or to make changes to it. Another countermeasure is to make sure that Blue Tooth is turned off, or if it is used, to not accept any new connection or pairing requests. If in doubt, deny permission if such a message appears on the phone. Another common sense counter measure is make sure that the Blue Tooth connection is set so that it is not discoverable. More information can be obtained by searching on-line for bluejacking and also for the term, bluesnarfing.

Another pitfall with cellular phones are the pictures that have been taken using them may have the G.P.S. co-ordinates of the location where the picture is taken. What this means is that phones that do this will give away the location of children or other family if a person knows what program to use to read the information embedded in the graphics file. Depending on the device, various types of information may be given away.

One way to help secure against unwanted surveillance is by removing applications that are not absolutely needed. Even after doing this, it is still possible for the spy part of the software to remain on the phone.

Computers

Computer and information security involves access control, and information access. By controlling, information can be kept out of the wrong hands. This means that confidential data should stay confidential. It also means that children or even adults can be prevented from accessing information that can cause them or the owner trouble. This includes preventing access to illegal file sharing sites, bomb making materials, pornography, etc.

Just as important as access control is reliable access to information stored on a computer. Information such as family pictures, music collections, business documents, medical records, etc. is no good if authorized users cannot get to the information when it is needed. Access to this type of information can be blocked temporarily or permanently due to hardware failure (such as hard drives malfunctioning), erasure or encryption (when authorized users have no access to or have forgotten the decryption keys). Access control will be discussed first and then reliable access will be discussed after.

When one has access to another's computer, that person also has access to much of that person's private life. Another thing to keep in mind is despite the fact that a computer may be protected with passwords or other access control devices, unsupervised physical access means that the person using the computer will have complete access to everything on the computer. Passwords can be easily cracked or sniffed by readily available software. Even worse is the possibility of malicious software being unknowingly downloaded. However, just about all of the risks can be reduced by simply using the tools presented elsewhere in this book. The virtualization programs allow separate operating systems to be run on the same computer at the same time.

If the guest operating system's

security is compromised, it will not in most cases, have a negative impact on the host operating system. Another way to minimize potential damage by malicious software is to create separate accounts on a computer for specific uses. These accounts should not have administrative privileges. In Windows, this can be done by opening the Control Panel and clicking on Users and then adding user accounts. One account can be used for social purposes and another used to conduct business. One should also ensure that at least one account with administrative privileges is accessible. Each account should also be password protected. If malicious software does manage to find its way on a computer, limited access should prevent it from taking over the entire system.

Another tactic that is used to keep computers secure is to update software frequently. Criminals who break into computer systems tend to take advantages of bugs or features in order to trick programs into giving up information or to execute malicious instructions. Many software writers and publishers try to correct these bugs or errors in order to make their software more secure. Doing this keeps their reputation intact and is the responsible thing to do. People should take advantage of the opportunity to keep the baddies off their systems.

Downloading software is one popular activity for many computer users. Downloaded software can contain malicious software, so a user should work to minimize risk. One way to do this is to not use the downloaded software right away. A user, if possible, should wait a couple of days before opening or installing downloaded programs. After waiting these two days, the user should update each antivirus program on his or her computer and then perform a scan on the file to be opened. Doing this will give anti virus makers time to update their definition databases to catch new malware just released.

Just as it is important for information owners to secure their information from unauthorized access, it is also important to make sure that information owners and authorized users have access to their information when and as needed.

There is a saying, "Don't put all your eggs in one basket." This saying is very applicable to information. Information of any importance should be put in the very minimum of two different baskets or in technical terms, media. It should be in preferably three.

There are several way of doing this. It is recommended that not only should the owner of information put his or her information on different media but that these media should be stored in separate places. If does no good to have a prefect backup of information stored on separate media when both the computer and backup media are in the same building and that building burns to the ground. Therefore, it is important to store at least one copy of important information at a separate location. It also does an information owner no good if a hard drive crashes and when he or she tries to recover important information from a backup finds that the backup media is also bad. This has happened quite a few times. It is important to periodically test that the backup media is in good condition and the media access device is in good functioning order.

One commonly overlooked item when it comes to backup up information are the programs or applications used to open up each type of information. Many people who are very careful to back up their data on a daily basis find out the hard way that they have neglected to keep a working copy of the programs used to access this information or any serial number or is needed to re-install such programs. They may end up having to buy a new copy of the program which may or may not be able to recognize older formats of the data that older the version were able to access. This was the case that happened with an author's client who was using Turbo Tax software. Fortunately, the author was able to locate and set up the older version of Turbo Tax so that the client was able to print out the needed tax information. People need to keep any original media as well as manuals or serial numbers necessary to re-install such software. People can also use mirror imaging software to make periodic backups of their hard drives. Two programs that do this are Norton Ghost which is available in most software supply stores or Clonezilla which is available as a free download from http://www.clonezilla.org/. Mirror imaging software should be run on computers storing important information before any new software is is installed and also after such software is installed and tested.

There are several types of media that can be used to backup important information. These include writable

CD's and DVD's, USB thumb drives, USB hard drives, on-line storage services, and the most reliable as far as access is concerned, plain old fashioned hard copy (paper). Each has its own advantages and disadvantages.

Writable CD'S and DVD'S are limited to the amount amount of information they can store. Several may be needed to backup information. In addition CD'S and DVD'S can deteriorate over time. They are also vulnerable to high temperatures. In the event of prolong power loss, such media is inaccessible until power is restored or alternative power is used.

CD'S and DVD'S are cheap to purchase and can be used to store many files. Rewritable CD'S and DVD'S are more expensive, but they can be reused several times. These

CD'S and DVD'S are usually labeled as CD-RW, CD+RW, DVD-RW, DVD+RW, or have the word, "rewritable" on the package.

USB thumb drives can hold various amounts of information. They are also very compact, portable, and relatively inexpensive (five to sixty dollars). Just about all of them can be carried on a person's key chain. They can also be easily hidden or stored in a secure location. The disadvantages include the fact that thumb drives can malfunction. They also deteriorate over time and do have a limited number of times they can be erased and rewritten (usually numbering in the hundreds of thousands of times).

External USB hard drives are reliable as internal computer hard drives. They can also store vast amounts of information. They, while not as inexpensive as thumb drives or CD/DVD media are still pretty affordable. One can find a 1 terabyte trillion bytes) drive for less than a hundred dollars. Even though they are affordable and store vast amounts of information, there are some disadvantages as well. A terabyte drive is about the size of a medium sized book. They are also relatively fragile. Even a fall from a height of two to three feet can cause such a drive to become inoperable. They too require power in order to access information that is stored on them.

One of the real up and coming methods of backup are the various on line backup services such as Mozy (http://www.mozy.com).

These services offer the the advantages of remote storage as well as likely being in a physically secure facility. There are also disadvantages to on-line backup. One disadvantage is the fact that there are recurring costs associated with such services. One also has to question what happens to the backed up information if someone forgets to pay the service fee. Another disadvantage is the fact that people using these services are dependent upon an outside organization. An even more pressing disadvantage is the fact that there is no access to the backed up information should the Internet be down. Also, the speed of backup and recovery depend heavily upon the speed of the networking infrastructure from the computer being backed up to where the backup information is being stored.

Out of all the information backup methods available, the most reliable is plain old fashioned paper (also known as hard copy). The advantages of paper include the fact that paper can last tens or even hundreds of years if properly stored. Information stored on paper does not need electricity to be access or viewed. Neither does it require any equipment except for maybe a pair of glasses. However, like other backup media, paper has disadvantages as well. Paper tend to take up lots of space. While it does store such formats as formatted information, text files and pictures, it cannot store many types of information such as video, audio, etc. Paper storage also can deteriorate over time. It is also difficult to convert from paper format back to digital formats.

Answering Machines

One common way of pilfering information include the telephone answering machine or combination type machines. Most answering machines have the capability of allowing incoming messages to be played back remotely by simply calling the line to which the answering machine is connected and punching in a code.

Unfortunately, in the vast majority of these machines, the "security" code is only two or three digits. There are computer programs free for the downloading that can play every combination of these tones in minutes allowing the correct code to be received by the answering machine. After the correct code is deduced, a person can then easily dial someone's answering machine and listen to the messages on it at any time. On such machines, it is best to disable remote message playback in order to prevent this from happening. If remote playback is considered necessary, one should consider using voice mail service provided by the phone company or setting up one's own voice mail program. If one has the time and inclination, there is a dedicated system that is completely free available on-line. One such program discussed in Chapter three is available   at http://www.asterisk.org.   Any system that does not allow at least a five digit authorization code should be considered insecure. The author prefers at least an eight digit access code. If the answering machine has no way of disabling the remote access feature and does not allow the setting of an adequately long access code, then it should be replaced. If a person is concerned about a governmental agency spying, then securing the answering machine against remote access may be a moot point since governmental agencies have wiretap powers.

Voice over I.P. Telephones

Voice Over I.P. (V.O.I.P.) or Internet telephones are a great way to save money on long distance calls, unfortunately, with the right equipment, it is sometime possible for unauthorized parties to be able to listen in on the conversations. The eavesdropper will either have to have access to the home or office network on which the V.O.I.P. telephone is installed and install monitoring software on a computer on the network. Some V.O.I.P. phones even allow access to place calls remotely. All an eavesdropper would have to do is log onto the phone's web interface and type in a phone number or V.O.I.P URL and click on "Call." The phone will then dial out, and if the eavesdropper's system is set up to answer right away, he or she can listen to what is happening in the room where the phone is located. This in and of itself illustrates the need to change default passwords to passwords that are hard to guess or crack.

Traditional Phones and Cordless Phones

Many warnings have been given about the insecurities of using the Internet to place and receive calls. Many problems also exist with the traditional telephone system as well. It is a trivial matter for an average person to be able to record telephone conversations. It is possible to do this with an inexpensive device called a "telephone recording device" combined with an inexpensive cassette recorder that has a microphone and remote input. Altogether, the price of these two devices can be as low as $35 especially if they are bought on-line. Using an additional telephone line splitter, it is possible to connect such a device by simply plugging it into the network interface device provided by the telephone company. The network interface device is the little box on the side of buildings to which telephone company lines are connected to the internal telephone wiring of the building. It is also possible, with a bit more knowledge, to tap into the telephone line at junction boxes or pedestals that are located on the side of the road.

Those who have concerns that such monitoring is happening should inspect the network interface device for any extra wires paying specially close attention to any wires that look similar to the cord that connects telephones to jacks on the wall. It is legal to open the network interface device as well in order to facilitate inspection.

Another item to check are the cordless phones located in the home. Since these phones use the airwaves to transmit conversations, it is possible for an eavesdropper to listen to conversations using a radio scanner tuned to the correct frequencies. Many late model cordless phone systems use technologies that help lessen the risk of unauthorized monitoring by such scanners, but the risk remains. When buying cordless phones, one should look for systems that employ digital encryption or at least spread spectrum (hopping different frequencies during the course of the conversation) technologies.

Home Security Devices

There are many types of devices available that allow people to monitor their homes and businesses. These devices include burglar alarms, video cameras, still cameras, driveway alarms, and even hidden microphones. While these can help in the capture of thieves and vandals, the same can also be bypassed and even used to spy on their owners. With proper consideration to the possibilities of such misuse, one can take proactive steps to prevent such from occurring.

One of the biggest protection industries is the home and small business burglar alarm industry.

Companies such as A.D.T. Guardian, and others install alarm systems in homes and businesses. They may make some money from installing and selling the equipment, but they also make money from providing a monitoring service. The monitoring service consists of telephone connected alarm receivers that decipher alarm signals when burglar alarms dial in to report a break in, employees who verify alarm condition, and the facilities in which these are housed.

In addition, most alarm system panels are not manufactured by the alarm companies such as A.D.T. but rather by electronic companies such as Honeywell. What this means is that with most alarm panels, it is not only possible to change service to a different monitoring service, but it is also possible for one to provide a self-monitored service. Self monitoring requires a computer program and an incoming telephone line (or V.O.I.P. trunk). The author provides his own self monitoring service for less than two dollars a month. There are professional alarm monitoring services available for less than nine dollars a month. One very good website that provides in-depth informations about do it yourself alarm installation and monitoring is http://www.diyalarmforum.com.

Common industry standard alarm panels have three main ways of contacting a monitoring station to report a break in. These include plain old telephone service, radio transmission (via cellular service or long range radio), and via the Internet. In any of these three cases, it is not a voice message that is transmitted but rather a series of audio tones or digital data. In the case of audio tones being used, the system dials a pre-programmed number and awaits a handshake tone from the monitoring service. When the handshake tone is heard, the alarm panel transmits a series of tones that communicate the type of alarm occurrence. The alarm panel then awaits a "kiss off" tone that indicates that the alarm data has been properly received. If this kissoff signal is received, the alarm panel "considers" the matter reported and does not make any more attempts to report the condition. One such alarm communication protocol is called, ContactID. ContactID uses touch tone signaling that is basically the same sounds made by dialing a number on a normal telephone. Other protocols are Ademco slow speed, Ademco fast speed, SIA, Acron Superfast, FBI Superfast, and many others. For the average user, unless he or she is programming his or her own alarm panel or setting up his or her own monitoring service, the communications channel (telephone, radio, or Internet) is the most important issue. Telephone or Internet provider cables can be cut or radio signals can be jammed. There are ways to mitigate the possibility of these channels of communications from being disrupted. One of the ways of preventing lines from being cut is by hiding cables or utility boxes from the view of would be burglars and providing decoy boxes. A search of a popular auction site such as E-Bay using the word, "N.I.D." will show pictures of several types of network interface devices. One should bid on one that looks similar to what telephone providers use in the area of installation. Once obtained, the diversion N.I.D. should be equipped with a small length of cable that looks similar to appearance to telephone company cable. This cable is then attached to the diversion N.I.D., and the other end is buried. Wires should also be attached that lead into the home or business. It is very important for this diversion to look like a real telephone company installation.

After the diversion is set up, the real N.I.D. can be hidden or camouflaged. There are several ways of doing this, and they include plants and trellises, fiberglass boulders (hollow that can be fitted over the real N.I.D.), and in some cases, even a five gallon bucket. In places where the entry points for such such utilities cannot be hidden, the owner should take measures to protect the equipment from tampering. One way to do this is to build a double enclosure around the N.I.D. or cable box. Both the inner enclosure and the outer enclosure should be equipped with a lock. The outer enclosure should also be equipped with a tamper sensor. The alarm panel should be programmed to send a tamper signal as soon as possible if the outer enclosure is breached. The inner enclosure should be built so that it is as strong and impervious as possible. This needs to be done in order to slow a would be burglar down enough so that he or she is likely to give up and flee.

Another weakness with burglar alarms is the the delay in response to the alarm. This delay is built into most alarm panels by the manufacturer in order to comply with standards meant to prevent wasted resources due to false alarms. When an entry door sensor is tripped, the alarm panel gives a minimum of thirty seconds for the user to enter a code to disarm the system.

Even if the correct code is not entered and the alarm sounds, it waits an additional fifteen seconds before attempting to contact the alarm monitoring station. This comes to a minimum of forty five seconds before an attempt is made to contact a monitoring service. If or when actual contact is made with the monitoring service, it will take an additional thirty to sixty seconds to place a call to verify the alarm.

Depending upon the monitoring company's procedures it will take an additional amount of time before the alarm company contacts law enforcement. If a non-entry delay sensor is tripped or if a panic or duress button or code is activated, the alarm panel may attempt to contact the monitoring station right away. The 45 second delay between breaking into an entryway and the alarm panel attempting to contact the monitoring company gives a burglar plenty of time to attempt to locate the alarm panel to disable it or to grab readily available valuable and leave.

The danger of an alarm panel being disabled can be mitigated in many ways. If the alarm panel is of the type that includes the keyboard and sounder in the control panel, then a remote keyboard or key chain remote should be used to disarm the alarm when entry is made. The control panel should then be either hidden or protected with a double enclosure in a similar manner as the network interface device in the previous paragraph. If the alarm control panel has a built in siren, and it is hidden or camouflaged, then its internal sounder should be unplugged or switched off, and a remote siren should be used. For alarm panels that are to be protected by an enclosure, the enclosure should be located in a locked room or closet that is protected by sensors that are programmed to trigger the alarm system immediately if they are faulted. The idea is to give the alarm panel as much time as possible to send a burglary signal to a monitoring station.

Another type of home or business security device is the video camera. Video cameras have become small, cheap, and widely available. Many of these types of cameras are of the wireless types. The cheaper ones usually transmit without encryption and can be picked up by any receiver that happens to be tuned to the camera's frequency. Someone with a cheap receiver can actually use a home owner's own cameras to see inside the home or business. This can provide a criminal with information that will make the job of committing a burglary, home invasion robbery, rape or murder much easier.

By monitoring a home owner's camera, a criminal can determine if a person is home, what type of valuables are in the camera's field of view, or if there are any unsecured points of entry. If these wireless cameras also have microphones, then conversations within range can also be monitored. Another type of camera is the Ethernet camera. These can be relatively secure if a strong password is used to guard against unauthorized viewing.

Another type of security camera is the traditional wired camera. These can be individually recorded via a VCR, or they can be connected to a dedicated D.V.R. (Digital Video Recorder). Many of these D.V.R.'s can be viewed on line, so it is important to password protect their access page with a strong password. D.V.R.'s are also good in the fact that many are capable of recording up to sixteen cameras at a time. Combined with other security equipment, they can be used to identify the bad guy. Sixteen channel D.V.R.'s are available on-line for as little as $340.00. Another type of camera that can be used to monitor unguarded construction sites, rural areas, or places where Internet or electricity may not be readily available is the wildlife camera. Wildlife cameras can be mounted or hidden so that they take still pictures of a monitored area. On some models, in order to prevent battery drain, the camera inside these units are not instantly active. They have to be triggered by movement, and the camera takes about six seconds before it becomes fully active. When this type of wildlife camera is used, care must be taken so that it is aimed at closed gates or where a potential thief will likely linger for a small period of time.   In addition, the camera should be of the type that uses infrared instead of a flash as a flash will give away the camera's position.

The camera can be camouflaged with foliage from around the area. After a period of time, the wildlife camera can be connected to a computer via a standard USB cable and the pictures taken can be browsed and saved. If one wants to monitor the area where a thief is likely to drive a vehicle to reach the site, one should be aware that most wildlife cameras take approximately six to ten seconds to be ready to take pictures.   If the owner of the site wants to monitor a drive way, he or she needs to keep vehicles in the monitoring area long enough for the camera to ready itself to take pictures.

One way to do this is to string a cable across the the area of travel. A gate will also work.   In cases where an owner cannot afford to buy or is unable borrow such equipment, the owner may decide to make signs stating that such cameras are hidden on the property. If really expensive equipment is to be protected, it can be protected with a prepaid G.P.S. telephone with tracking enabled. Instructions on how to do this and what phones work with such services can be found at http://www.mologogo.com.

Wireless Routers

Wireless routers make installing

computer local area networks relatively easy. This is due to the fact that no wires need to be run in order to facilitate communications between computers in a home or business. Wireless routers also provide a degree of protection against lightning strikes. However, if not properly configured wireless networks can easily expose a gaping security hole that allows any nearby computer equipped with a wireless card to easily sign onto a network or to intercept communications between computers. Fortunately, it is relatively easy and inexpensive to make such access impractical to all but the most determined snoop. Most routers have the ability to be set up to encrypt all communications that occur over a wireless connection. Each device on the network, including the router must have the same type of encryption set up. In addition, each device must also have the same network key entered. Two of the most popular forms of encryption include WEP (Wired Equivalent Protocol) and WPA (Wi-Fi Protected Access). While WEP is in a few cases better than nothing at all, it is still relatively insecure, and the key can be deduced by intercepting wireless traffic. It usually can be done within anywhere from a few minutes to a few hours. Another thing that needs to be done is to change the default password that is required in order to configure the router. If the default password is left in place a piece of malicious software can easily turn off wireless, encryption or in some cases expose the encryption key so that it can be used by an attacker. The new password chosen should be at least eight characters long and include capital letters, lowercase letters, numbers, and punctuation. This password should be written down and stored in a secure area. Some people actually write the password on a sticky note and put this on the bottom of the router.

It is not recommended that this be done unless the router is located in a secure area. Another way to hide a network from potential intruders is to prevent the network identification or SSID (Service set identifier) from being broadcast. Doing this will not totally eliminate the possibility of intruders from identifying a wireless network, but it will make the network harder for them to detect. However, it will also make it more difficult for new devices to be connected to the same network. One other thing that needs to be mentioned is the fact that most wireless routers' capabilities can be upgraded on-line. In fact, most routers have an "upgrade firmware" option contained in their configuration menu. When upgrading a router, one must be sure to carefully follow instructions provided, or one may end up with a paper weight. A botched firmware upgrade can render a router useless. Fortunately, most routers do have safety features built in to prevent this from happening. Upgraded firmware can cure problems such as lost connections, weak encryption, and add more capabilities such as filtering.

If an unsecured wireless router is being configured to provide encryption, it may be a good idea to change the SSID or network name before the router is restarted. This is due to the fact that client computers may try to connect to the router using the previous connection properties.

On some computers, it may be very

easy to change these properties. However, on others, it may be more difficult. Filtering capabilities can protect computers from users who download malicious executable files.

However, these same filters can also prevent the computer and programs from receiving automatic software updates. If filtering is used, one should do a test by trying to update their anti-virus definition database after such filtering is activated. If filtering does cause problems, it can be turned of periodically so that virus definitions can be manually updated. It is also possible for many routers to be set up to filter and log access to undesirable content such as pornography, bomb making, and "hacking" tutorials. When one does this to protect family or business, one should be aware that it is in most cases possible for another person to bypass the router by plugging a network cable directly into the broadband modem. If this happens, the router and all of its protections are taken out of the picture.

In most cases, it is also possible to reset the router by pressing and holding a reset button while the router is powered off and back on. If this is done, the user who is trying to bypass a router's filter now has full access to reconfigure the router. If a user has physical access to the router he or she can actually unplug the Ethernet cable (if using a wired connection) that goes to his or her computer from the router and plug it directly into the cable modem for temporary unauthorized access if nobody else is using the network. Fortunately, if the router is located in a locked area, these types of attack can be made much more difficult.

Routers can definitely be use to provide both security and convenience for both home and business owners as long as the person setting up the router is aware of a few facts.

Home Entertainment Devices

Many home entertainment devices have the option of being connected to the Internet or in the case of some satellite receivers, can be plugged into a phone line. One use for such a feature is to allow the ordering of pay per view movies or to download files that add or delete capabilities from the receiver.

Unfortunately, this also gives home entertainment devices the opportunity to "phone home" with information on viewing habits. The author keeps his Dish Network satellite receiver unplugged from the phone line. The only time it is plugged in is when a pay per view movie is to be ordered.

Radio Frequency Identification (R.F.I.D.)

Radio frequency identification chips are becoming widespread. These miniature transceivers work by using a very small pickup coil in which electric current is induce by a nearby R.F.I.D. scanner. The power from that miniature coil is used to power a microscopic radio transmission circuit. This circuit transmits a digital signal back to the R.F.I.D. scanners. R.F.I.D. tags and chips are used for many things such as inventory, security, access control, information transmission (bank cards passports, etc.), and location detection. R.F.I.D. use has serious privacy implications.

When R.F.I.D. chips are encoded with unique numbers or personal identification, people can be tracked or in the case of R.F.I.D. equipped passports, identities stolen. R.F.I.D. tags can be found in certain brands of clothing, U.S. passports, credit cards, and many other common household items. For credit cards, passports, and other items containing R.F.I.D. chip containing personal information, measures should be taken to protect personal identity information. Credit cards that have "wave and pay," "touch and go,"

"Speed Pass," or similar methods of contactless credit card payments are embedded with R.F.I.D. chips. R.F.I.D. chips' transmissions can be shielded by enclosing the items containing the chip inside a metal enclosure. This can be done by wrapping credit cards or passports with aluminum foil. Another method that can be used is buying a metal cigarette case to enclose such items. One enterprising individual has made protective wallets using duct tape and aluminum foil. For those who are really cautious may request cards that do not have R.F.I.D. chips embedded. The ultra-paranoid or extremely curious person can purchase an R.F.I.D. scanner over the Internet.

G.P.S. Navigation

G.P.S. Saves time and money by allowing people to quickly reach their destination without having to spend time and gas driving around looking for their destination. G.P.S. stand for Global Positioning System. It works on a network of satellites sending beacon data towards earth at predetermined intervals. This data is sent by each satellite in a network at almost exactly the same time.

Each satellite transmission includes a time stamp and information identifying from which satellite the transmission came. By comparing the time stamp of transmission and actual arrival time of the transmission, a small computer in the G.P.S. can determine the distance from each satellite. When the G.P.S is able to determine its distance from three or more satellites, it can then use mathematics to calculate its location. This information is used to determine latitude and longitude. The G.P.S. is then able to access its internal database to show a map, points of interests, as well as the addresses of homes, businesses, and other facilities. In after market G.P.S. Navigation devices such as Tom Tom, Garmin, and many other brands, this information is displayed on a screen and is contained within the G.PS. device itself. None of this information is transmitted to cell phone companies, government agencies, etc. There are other devices that are capable of transmitting such information, and these include dealer installed options such as On Star navigation systems, G.P.S. surveillance devices, smart phones etc. Even though this is the case, it is still possible to use a G.P.S. navigation unit to track where one has been and when. This is due to the fact that these devices can and do log location data. On some units, this can be seen by the fact that a road color on a map may be a different color if the route has been previously traveled. Such G.P.S. logs can and have been used in divorce cases and to catch cheating spouses. These log files should be cleared periodically if one desires to protect privacy. A search on the Internet for the model number of the G.P.S. unit and the words, "log file" or "track log" should turn up information on how to delete and or make use of these files. Imagine how much money can be saved in lawyers fees or how much can be made in a divorce or lawsuit. To access the Garmin brand G.P.S. unit's log file, one needs to use a USB cable to plug the unit into a computer. The computer will recognize the unit as a new removable drive. Open the My Computer (Computer for Windows 7 and Vista) and click on the icon that has the name of the G.P.S. unit. Once that is done, open the G.P.S. folder. The file, current.gpx, contains the human readable log of where the unit has traveled (G.P.S. co-ordinates) and the time (UTC not local time) each entry is made. IF the file is deleted, the unit will create a new (blank) one when it is restarted. It is best to make a backup of this file just in case. This file is created and updated even if the logging features are turned off.

If one is not able to locate information on how to delete log files, the G.P.S. unit can be left at home if privacy is such a concern. There are devices on-line that will jam G.P.S. signals. Before buying such a device, one should check to make sure that the use of such a device is legal in the area where it is to be operated.

G.P.S. navigation units can also help protect people against legalized robbery such as speed traps, red light cameras, speed cameras, and other devices used by law enforcement to separate drivers from their money. There are companies that collect information from users regarding locations used as speed traps. This information is submitted to the company's website, and is vetted by other users. The companies compile such information into what are called points of interests files.

These files can be downloaded to navigation units. Units that have such downloaded data can warn drivers when they are approaching such areas. One company called, Phantom Alert sells such data. While this data can be viewed on-line in a map for free by visiting http://www.phantomalert.com, it costs money to be able to download the data to a G.P.S. or smart phone. The price varies from a few dollars to one hundred dollars for a lifetime membership. Trapster is another website that allows speed trap and automated ticketing device locations to be downloaded for free is http://www.trapster.com. The

Trapster database uses data inputted by drivers. G.P.S. alerts show the status of the alert, who contributed the data, and when the data was collected.

If even one traffic ticket is avoided by using one of these, this book will pay for itself. Just an additional note:

License plate covers or sprays that claim to block traffic enforcement cameras do not work. This was tested on the Myth Busters show, and they all failed to block the cameras from being able to record the number.

Physical security involves more than locking doors and windows. It also involves keeping track of property as well as keeping loose lips closed. Many con artists and other thieves can glean personal information just by observation and in may cases, by simply knowing how to ask for it.

Bank Cards

Debit and credit cards are a convenient way to make purchases without carrying cash. If lost or stolen, they can be canceled. Unfortunately, thieves have also come up with innovative ways to steal money using information about debit and credit cards.

One innovative way of obtaining credit card information involves a technique called, "phishing." Phishing occurs when a victim is tricked into revealing information on real looking but fake websites. The link to such a website may be advertised in an email, or it may appear on a search for a product. It also may show up as a result of malicious software embedded on a computer. Users should never enter credit or debit card information into any website provided in an email. In fact, users should not use a debit card for any on-line transaction as it is much more to recover funds that may be stolen via fraud.

Another technique used to steal debit or credit card information involves using a device called a skimmer. A skimmer is a device that fits over the slot of an ATM machine or credit card terminal. When the user inserts or swipes his or her debit or credit card, the skimmer record the information contained in the magnetic strip embedded in the card. If a security code is needed, a near by camera can be used to see what number is entered.

There are several counter measure that can be used to protect one's self from skimming. On machines where the card is inserted, a person can lightly tug on anything protruding around the slot where the card is inserted. If perts come off, they are likely part of a skimming device. Another method of protection is to cup one's hand around the keyboard used to enter security codes and use the body to shield the keypad from cameras or onlookers.

Another method used by thieves to steal money involves tampering with credit card terminals or ATM machines. One such technique involves the insertion of an object into the slot of the terminal or ATM that causes the victim to be unable to withdraw a card. Once the victim leaves the machine, the thief is able to remove the card and use it to purchase merchandise or steal money.

A variation of this technique involves the thief gluing the ENTER and CANCEL keys on the ATM or terminal that has a touch screen so that the victim, after entering his or her security code, cannot withdraw funds or make a purchase. After the victim leaves the machine, the thief uses the touch screen to complete the entering of the security code so that money can be withdrawn.

There are three techniques that can be used to protect against theft by tampering. With one, the potential victim can check to see if there is a touch screen on the ATM or credit card terminal and use it (if available) to complete the transaction. The user can also closely examine the card slot to see if there are any objects protruding from the card slot or if there is any tape near the slot before attempting to insert a card. If a card is already stuck, the user should check again for any such protrusion. If there are, the user should attempt to lightly pull on it to see if the card come out. The other technique involves a little preparation. People should carry the telephone number of the issuing company for all cards whenever the cards are carried. This way, the user can contact the credit or debit card issuing company before leaving the ATM or credit card terminal. The issuing company may render the card useless while it is still stuck in the machine.

Except for cash withdraws, credit cards should be used rather than debit cards when conducting business. This is due to the fact that credit cards usually provide better protection in the event of a theft. The user can pay the amount that normally would have been put on the debit card right away in order to avoid usury.

Credit Bureaus

Credit bureaus make money by determining credit ratings of people and companies and reporting this information to those who pay for it. Because of abuses in how these reporting companies collect, handle, trade, and sell private information, people have fervently demanded that the government pass laws to protect data against misuse. These laws make it mandatory for credit reporting companies to provide one free yearly credit report a year for each person who requests it. In addition, credit reporting companies are also required to provide a report when a person is denied credit. Many of these companies make additional money by also offering "identity protection" services for a charge.

This type of protection would not be needed if governments and big business had not forced people to have numbers attached to their lives. Unfortunately, we the people have no choice in this matter without severely disrupting our own lives and this country. However, there is an option available that will allow people to protect their identities without having to pay monthly fees. This option is known as a "credit freeze." A credit freeze prevents inquiries into their credit record. A person who wants to initiate a credit freeze must come up with an access code that only he or she can remember. This code must be provided should the person want to "thaw" his or her credit report so that he or she can get a car or home loan, etc. There may be a charge for freezing or thawing the credit information, but it is very likely that these charges will be much less than what will be incurred for buying identity theft insurance.

Releasing Information

Many people will provide information to callers based upon caller identification information displayed on phones and information provided by the caller. They do this without realizing that Caller ID information can be faked. It is very easy for someone to set the caller identification so that it shows the telephone number (and name) of a bank and then to call a victim. The con man will then ask for personal information in order to "verify" the identity of the account holder. Once enough personal information is extracted from a victim, identity theft can occur. The victim is the one who has to clean up his or her credit and try to recover stolen funds. Another form of fraud is for a con man to set up an anonymous toll free telephone number and then send a convincing "offer" or bargain through the mail.

This "offer" may contain the logo and letterhead of a bank or other company with which the victim does business. When the victim calls in to sign up for the "offer," the con man will then ask for account information to "verify identity" of the victim. The account information is then used to siphon funds or order merchandise.

When one receives offer in the mail or calls from someone claiming to represent a company, one should call the company using **only** the telephone number on record for the bank or company. Such information can be found on account statements. If such information is unavailable, the phone book should be used to look up the correct telephone number or a local branch of the company or bank should be called. The toll free number contained in any offer whether by telephone or mail should **not** be verified by searching the Internet unless the information is obtained from a website **already known** to belong to the bank or company in question.

This is due to the fact that it is relatively easy to set up a web site that imitates the bank or company in question. It is also easy to get any telephone number listed on on-line databases.

Access Control Devices

Access control devices are just what the name implies. They are devices that control access to a certain area or resource. In other words, an access control device is a fancy word for a lock. Access control devices range from the very simple mechanical pad lock to the complex such as fingerprint scanners. Many access control devices may seem impervious to many people but may actually be quite easy to bypass. Since this is a book about technology and saving money, security technology, both electronic and mechanical are discussed in order to help protect money and assets. In many cases, it is not necessary to spend a lot of money to get good security.

Many home and business owners spend hundreds of dollars on high security locks only to overlook the gap between double doors. In cases where there there is a thumb turn on the inside, a thief can insert a stiff, bent rod between the doors in order to turn the thumb turn and unlock the door. Such an event can be prevented with a simple metal plate that covers the gap between the doors. This is the case where money overrules common sense. When one wants to upgrade security, one should try to think like a thief ans ask, "How would I break in or get around this security product?"

Warded locks should **not** be used as a theft prevention device. In most cases, these are trivial to pick or to open with an improvised key. These type of locks are one of the most ancient type of lock. They can be identified by the type of key they use. Warded locks have keys that have notches that are cut straight into the blade of the key. They may, however be used for certain safety situations such as on cabinets where cleaners and other poisons may be stored.

Pin tumbler locks are used on most homes and businesses. These locks can provide relatively decent security. However, with the proliferation of of lock picking and lock bumping manuals both on-line and in stores as well as the easy availability of lock picks, the security of the average pin tumbler locks has been diminished somewhat.

To maintain security, pick resistant locks are needed. Pick resistant locks are now sold in most major hardware chains as well as in locksmithing establishments. Locks with pick resistant tumblers are usually only a few dollars more expensive than their less resistant counterparts. Pick resistant locks take much more time to pick than their non pick resistant counterparts. Locks that are pick resistant will usually have print on the packaging saying that they are pick resistant or they will say that they contain spool tumblers or mushroom pins.

Remote entry key fobs are very popular. Some of these devices can be easily cloned. Others are not so easy to clone. Remote key chain fobs offer a convenient way to enter buildings, cars, or to turn off alarm systems. The ones that are hard to clone offer reasonable security. Sometimes, one key fob can be used to control multiple devices.

Keypad entry control is used on many type of locks from those on car to those in the home and even in many businesses. Many of these keypad provide decent security. They should be capable of being programmed with a bare minimum of four digits for the combination. Users should also avoid using a combinations consisting of single numbers such as 1111, 4444, etc.

One should periodically clean the keys or buttons found on these devices and replace any key or button that looks worn. Dirty or worn buttons provide potential thieves clues to the combination. If for some reason the buttons or keys cannot be replaced or cleaned, the combination should be changed so that non worn or dirty keys are used.

Biometric devices such fingerprint scanners are being seen more and more often on computers as well as building with higher grade security.

Finger print readers provide reasonably good security, but they can be fooled. When someone uses a finger print scanner, that person leaves a finger print behind. If that finger print is lifted, it can be used to create a copy that can be used to fool the scanner at a later time. There are many web sites that provide instructions on how to fool a finger print scanner. The TV show, Myth Busters, made an episode on how to fool finger print scanners using methods found on many of these websites. Each scanner that was tested was able to be fooled.

Barcode Scanners have been use in the work place for many years. They are used both for time recording as well as access control. Barcode scanners provide relatively little in the way of security due to the fact that barcodes can be photocopied or read and regenerated with commonly available, free programs such as Zbar and Zint. A micro camera or another video recording device can actually store a picture of a barcode, and there are many cellphones that can read barcodes as well.

Some R.F.I.D. (Radio Frequency Identification) scanners provide good security so long as they are not vulnerable to being cloned or spoofed. Cloning involves making a R.F.I.D. tag that not only looks the same but also transmits the same tag id number when queried. Cloning is very difficult. Spoofing involves the interception of a R.F.I.D. chip's signal. This signal is recorded and retransmitted to gain unauthorized entry. Spoofing equipment is more bulky than the corresponding R.F.I.D. tag. However, in many cases, a deactivated R.F.I.D. tag can be used for the looks and spoofing equipment can be used to reproduce the R.F.I.D. signal. Another vulnerability exists where an authorized person may be able to enter a controlled area outside of the time frame where he or she is granted access. This problem results from both poor system programming and improper installation of R.F.I.D. scanners. If a R.F.I.D. scanner that allows exit from a controlled area is located close enough for it to be operated by a R.F.I.D. tag from outside of the controlled area, it is possible for someone to trigger the exit R.F.I.D. scanner in order to unlock the door. The system is fooled into allowing the door to be open so that the tag holder can "exit" the controlled area. Proper shielding and programming can be used to prevent such unauthorized re-entry.

Voice print locks works by listening for

the unique voice characteristics of people authorized to access protected area. Voice print locks can sometimes be spoofed by using a digital or high quality analog recorder.

Iris scanners are one of the most secure forms of access control devices. They work by recording the unique characteristics of each authorized person's iris. These characteristics are stored in a database, and when someone requests access, their iris characteristics are compared to the characteristic of authorized people. If there is a match, the person is granted access. These devices are very hard to spoof at the time this book is written. Unfortunately, iris scanning devices are also very expensive.

Exit buttons or bars are used to allow

people to easily exit a building or controlled area in the event of a fire or other emergency where it is necessary to quickly evacuate a building. These devices can also be used to allow unauthorized entry into a controlled area. If an unauthorized person can insert a rod, stiff wire or any other object between a door frame and the door itself, it may be possible to operate the latch and cause the door to be opened.

Electromechanical latches are used to allow a person or device to "buzz in" a visitor. The device works by releasing the strike plate on the side of a door. In many cases, such a latch is improperly installed and will allow an intruder to insert an object to either leverage the latch or to push in a retractable bolt in order to allow unauthorized entry. The best way to guard against this type of unauthorized entry is to use a metal plate that covers the latch as well as the lock's bolt. Another method that works is by installing the door to the controlled area so that it opens inward and installing the electromechanical latch on the inside. This limits exposure of the latch or bolt to outside intruders.

Securing and Documenting Items

Home and business security should be more than locks and alarms. In many cases, locks and alarms will discourage vandalism and theft. However, this is not always the case. There are many burglars who specialize is smash and grab types of behavior. This means that they smash in a door or window and grab as many items that they can get a hold of in less than a minute or two. In cases like this, the thieves are long gone by the time an alarm monitoring service is able to notify anyone that the break in occurred. The good news is the fact that even a smash and grab job can be made more difficult with a little forethought.

Big ticket items can be secured with eye bolts, chains, and padlocks. They can also be secured with security cables made especially for this purpose. While such cables can be cut or pried loose, they will slow down the burglar. A burglar is usually under pressure to complete a theft as quickly as possible in order to avoid being caught. When a burglar is slowed down, he or she may steal fewer items or he or she may get greedy enough to spend more time on the job and get caught. If the victim's site has an alarm that has successfully notified people of the burglary in progress then there is the chance that the burglar may be caught in the act. Small items can be kept under lock and key, or they can be cleverly hidden. For about forty five bucks, one can equip a closet door with dead bolt that requires a key to open. This may be a very good place to store small valuables if they have to be kept at home.

In instances where burglars are able to make away with items, steps should be taken to make it possible identify such items so that they may be returned if found. This can be done in numerous ways. One way to do this is to inventory all items in the home or business to be protected. The inventory should include pictures, the brand, model number, and serial number of each item. In cases where there is no serial number, a unique number can be engraved on such an item. This number should be recorded in the inventory as a special marking.

In many cases, items stolen are sold in order to finance drug habits. In many states, there are laws requiring pawn shop owners to require positive identification from anyone who pawns items. In these states, most have regulations requiring pawn shop owners to document any serial and model number of items. This information can then be compared to information in police databases regarding stolen items. If an item matches, the criminal can then be identified and hopefully, the items returned to their rightful owner. A victim of a burglary intent on locating their stolen items can and should do some detective work to see if their items are being sold. One such market place to check is the popular auction websites such as E-bay.

Another good place to check is free advertising sites such as Craig's list (http://www.craigslist.com). In addition, one can and should check local flea markets and thrift stores. Another option is using the ability to render stolen items useless. Many items that require subscription to services can be rendered useless upon theft. Items such as satellite receivers, cellular phones, pagers, as well as other items can be rendered useless by the companies providing service. To utilize this anti-theft tactic requires a bit of pre-planning. This pre-planning requires the owner of the equipment to read the owner's manual, make records of the model number, serial numbers, their electronic equivalents as well as the customer service number of the corresponding service providers. This information should be kept in safe places in both the home and car.

Some devices even allow their disabling via a simple text message or visit to a website. If this information on disabling and tracking any attempted use of a stolen device is kept handy, there is a higher possibility of recovery. Things that have serial and model numbers include cars, cameras, firearms, computers, e-readers, phones, cell phones, satellite receivers, stereos, iPods, iPads, and most any other device whether it uses high technology or not.

Avoiding Scams and Ripoffs

Scams and ripoffs can be found nearly everywhere, and this includes those which are advertised in TV. Many people who will discount the email scam that tells them they have won millions from some dictator will easily fall prey to the get rich quick scheme being offered on TV. The main difference between the two scammers is the fact that the one on TV can afford to pay the high advertising rate where the email scammer relies on cheaper means of advertising. When one is interested in checking out the latest TV get rich quick scheme, he or she should get on the Internet and search the name of the scammer or title of the scam. If still interested in getting the material, the potential victim can usually order the material very cheap on line from previous

victims. Many times, people who have ordered the material advertised will sell such material on places such as http://www.ebay.com for a very cheap price or in order to try to recoup some of their investment or to use the cheap price as a form of protest to being ripped off. Paying a dollar for worthless junk or information is much better than getting taken for tens or hundreds of dollars. One can also find many of these materials on peer to peer file sharing sites as well. Another place to investigate potential rip offs is http://www.ripoffreports.com.

People who get taken by unscrupulous businesses should try to get the business to make amends, and if the business does not budge, then a report to Rip Off Reports should be filed to make others aware of the issue. This may or may not get a person's money back, but it will help protect others. Then again, the business may decide that such a report remaining unsettled will possibly hurt sales and decide to make amends. However, there is good advice in order to prevent one's self from being defrauded.

When considering the purchase of any

scheme or course that teaches one how to make money in the stock market, dealing with foreclosure properties, etc. one should keep in mind that most of these programs are money losers and fail much more often than they are successful. Just think about it, if these schemes actually worked, the people teaching these courses would be making millions or billions working their program rather than teaching the program to others. Like the old adage says, "If it is too good to be true, than it is probably not."

http://www.zabasearch.com

Chapter 10 - Researching and Finding Information

Much information can be found on-line for just about any different topic. Unfortunately, with so many people trying to make a quick buck using the Internet, good information can be very hard to come by. When searching on-line using Google or any other search engine, a potential good result when clicked can lead a user to what is commonly referred to as a pay wall. In other words, the web site's teaser showed up in the results of a search, but once a user arrives at the site, he or she is required to provide payment or personal information in order to access the wanted information. This is becoming increasingly common. This chapter will show a user how to cut through the chase and get to the gems.

Finding people

Finding people is a hot topic when it comes to searches, and there are plenty of individuals and companies who are willing to scam people out of their hard earned money using deceptive or misleading advertising. Companies or individuals purporting to sell private cell phone records or unlisted numbers should be especially suspect. Fortunately, there are a number of free ways to attempt to locate a particular subject (target of the search). Many free search engines for locating people will provide information that is publicly available. However, when no information is available, these websites will provide a link to paid people search services. A few pretty good free nation wide people search engines are listed below:

http://www.anywho.com/

http://www.whitepages.com/

http://www.yellowpages.com

http://www.zabasearch.com/

The author has tried several different paid search services only to be provided useless information. People using paid search sites should be aware that in many cases, **they are paying for the search service rather than results**. This means that one will have to pay for the search even if there is no useful information delivered. A person who is thinking about using a paid search engine should head over to http://www.ripoffreport.com and enter the name of the search company or website and see what pops up.

One paid search engine that seems to be totally legitimate is http://www.salesgenie.com. Salesgenie offers a three day trial, and this trial does not require a credit card number or any payment information for the trial period. It does however, require the potential subscriber's name, address, business telephone number, and email address to sign up for the trial. The author entered his Yahoo email information. It was accepted, and the author, expecting to find a verification email, attempted to sign into Yahoo only to find the email account inactive. The author was still able to log into Salesgenie and do a lookup of several people and was able to verify accuracy of the information.

Another way of attempting to locate

information on a person is to type the name of the person inside a set of quotation marks into the the input of any search engine. If that fails or if there is an overload of information, then good places to try are social networks. Many people who have unlisted telephone numbers and attempt to keep them off the rest of the Internet seem to be willing to provide such information on their social networking accounts.

Some people on social networks tend to allow only friends to view their personal information, so a friends request may be in order. Some popular social networks to check are listed below:

http://www.facebook.com

http://www.linkedin.com

http://www.myspace.com

http://www.ning.com/

http://www.twitter.com

Another way to find personal information is by using government licensing databases. People employed in various occupations and professions are often required by state or federal government to have licenses. Many of these databases are open for search by the public. To search such databases and websites one should use a search engine and search for the name of the state and the words, "public record." An example of this is to search for Florida public records one would use the following term, *"Florida Public Record."*

Finding or Tracing Numbers

Many people get pesky calls where once answered, there is silence on the other end. These types of calls are known as "ghost calls." Ghost calls occur for several reasons. One reason is that the caller wants to determine of someone is home on a specific day and time. This type of information is especially useful for bill collectors and burglars. For bill collectors, knowing when their quarry is home will give them better opportunities for collection calls. For burglars, knowing when their quarry is not home will give them opportunities to break in and steal.

Fortunately, for those who are the subject of ghost calls, there is a tool that will allow those being called to get information on the caller. As big companies share data about customers, customers are returning the favor. One good website for tracking down toll free and other numbers is http://www.whocalled.us. A paid site that provides information can be found at http://www.cnam.info. This site also offers the option of looking up a limited amount of numbers for free. Another site that allows a person to look up the phone service provider as well as the city and state where a number is provisioned is http://www.nationalnanpa.com/na s/public/assigned_code_query_ste p1.do? method=resetCodeQueryModel.

One does not need to know the state where the call originates. For some reason, the form requires a state to be chosen, but it does not matter which state is chosen for the number lookup to succeed. Once the area code is entered, the user will see a list of telephone number prefixes, the city to which these prefixes are assigned, and the telephone service provider on record.

Finding information on-line can be a daunting task these days. This is due to the fact that owners of web sites which sell products try to game the search system so that the first result show their websites rather than the free information for which the user is looking.

The format in which a term is typed into the search box of a search engine can matter greatly. For example, the use of multiple words in a search query may yield results showing pages that contain just one of these words, pages that contain both words but in different parts of the page, or may contain results for the exact words as typed in. If a user is looking for pages containing the exact phrase, it is sometimes necessary to put the phrase within quotation marks.

If searching for a specific type of file use the *"filetype:"* specification. For example, if searching for a dog breeding e-book, the user may want to search using the terms *"Dog Breeding filetype:pdf."* Every decent search engine offers options that allow users to narrow their search to specific information. It pays for users to familiarize themselves with these options.

One good way to search for information is to use multiple search engines. Each search engine has a different method for ranking pages. People or companies wishing to be at the top of search engine results for specific keywords will often use search engine optimization techniques to achieve this. In many cases, they will even create a number of different websites specifically designed to produce high rankings for individual keywords. Fortunately for a person trying to find information, each search engine uses different methods to rank pages. Some of the various general search engines are listed below:

http://www.ask.com

http://www.altavista.com

http://www.google.com

http://www.webcrawler.com

http://www.yahoo.com

For searching for files available on FTP servers, one will have to have the

name of the file being sought and
then enter it into one of the following
search engines:

http://www.filesearching.com

http://www.filewatcher.com

Newsgroup search engines are also
available. Two good ones are listed
below:

http://www.binsearch.info

http://www.searchbin.net

Chapter 11 - Money Making Opportunities

There are plenty of money making opportunities when it comes to using a computer or any other related high technology device. Some of these have already been discussed in this book. The trick to making money with high technology is steering clear of the widely advertised money making scams.

In order to make money, one needs to find what he or she likes to do and what he or she is good at doing. In addition, one needs to do home work to find out what is profitable and what is not. When someone is the go to person for any type of situation, then that is what he or she is good at doing. Almost every self made millionaire has done what he or she has a passion for doing. Some suggestions are listed in this chapter.

Authoring

Writing books has made many people fortunes. This, however is not the case for most authors, especially if one book is not a seller, they quit trying. With new trends in electronic and self publishing, more people get to be heard. People considering writing a book should write about the topics in which they are knowledgeable. Even a quarterly newsletter can bring someone money especially if it contains topics in which people are interested. It also may help to submit articles to trade magazines.

Authors, when writing books, should consider more than one platform for selling their work. Traditional books are still sold in every town in the United States. Electronic books are also very popular. In fact, one author, Amanda Hocking, is a very successful author on the Kindle platform. She has sold hundreds of thousand of copies of her vampire book on-line. This was after traditional Twentieth Century publishers rejected her work. When it comes to authoring books, one should consider many different platforms for sales.

Publishing

Publishing is one area where a small producer can make good money. Publishing can be successful in many areas. Some of these areas include web design, booklets, news letters, and even business cards.

Those good at graphics design may

engage in web design. Web design is as much of an art as it is a science. Many local businesses do not have web site nor the know how to create them. A good Internet presence may help increase business for local companies. This is especially true of the web designer also has experience in promoting the created site.

Even if the publications are free, money can be brought in from advertisement. Local businesses may be persuaded to buy advertisements in small how-to type booklets. An example of such a booklet is mobile home repair. Another example is local do it yourself weed or pest control. Yet another example includes gardening or home maintenance. Booklets can be produced and sold for cheap, and once people see good information in them, they may be willing to pay a few dollars for them.

Advertising

Advertisement is another area where a small business can fill a niche. This is especially true for those who can come up with entertaining videos or podcasts. It is also true for those who know how to design eye catching signs. In order for a small business or advertising service to rise above the rest, it must use innovative techniques to catch the eyes or ears of the public. Another way for people to break into advertising is to use social networks to target advertisements to specific users in specific locations. For example, one could target local people who just got engaged for advertisements related to video production service for weddings.

Producing Videos

Video production is another area where a small business can make a buck. Many people who get married wish to record their weddings on video. Many places of worship may also be in the market for the video recording for their services. High quality video can be edited with free or very cheap software, and DVD's can be produced very inexpensively. A video production service may even offer on-line posting so that people can see the results relatively quickly. Those who are artistic may want to look into video production.

Selling On-line

Selling products on-line is another area where many people make a good living. With auction sites and on-line retail markets such as E-Bay, uBid, Amazon, Craig's List as well as others being popular, one can make money with things bought in yard sales or even with things that are thrown away. It is true that one man's junk is another man's treasure. Even home made articles such as screen printed t-shirts can fetch a handy profit.

Researching Information

Researching information is another way to make money. Many companies need market research. Even many high school or college students are willing to pay money for research that will bring in good grades. Some individuals or companies may be looking for a specific item to buy or may need to find a buyer for an item currently on hand. With the wide availability of the Internet, it is possible to match a seller and a buyer, for a fee, or course. There are other people who would like to reconnect with lost friends or loved ones. This is also an opportunity for a savvy researcher.

Computer Repair

Computer repair is also a good avenue for those with the technical knowledge to do this. A computer repair shop can be set up cheaply, and many tools used for repairing computers can be had for very cheap or even for free. A computer repair technician should be proficient in both hardware and software aspects of computers. Honest prices, good work, and quick turn around are something many people will appreciate.

Journalism

An investigative journalist is a rare

breed these days. It can also be dangerous work at times. However, people like to read stories about government or corporate corruption. With today's technology, it is very easy to make a video recording of a person or situation without the knowledge of the targeted individual. A small video recorder carried in a shirt pocket or disguised as a pen can record hours of footage. When a reporter gets the inside story enough times, people are willing to read or watch the channel whether it is on-line or in print. This is also a good avenue to attract advertisers.

Teaching

Teaching is another avenue where money can be made. People can teach others how to use a computer, play a musical instrument, learn a foreign language or any other topic.

Computers can be used to produce teaching aids and tools that will facilitate learning.

These are just a few of many money making opportunities that technology can bring about. Whatever one like to do, he or she needs to do the homework, find the market, and fill the niche. A small company or individual can compete with a larger company that has grown complacent. Bureaucracy slows initiative and innovation, and this gives the small producer a leg up.

Chapter 12
Miscellaneous Hacks

These are tips that cannot be classified under other categories. These include the mundane as well the interesting.

Bypass the Phone Tree

Most people hate calling a company only to have their call answered by a machine instructing them to press this and that button in order to reach a person. Many times people will press 0 continuously in order to get a person. Sometimes this will work, and sometimes it won't. There is a website, however, that has instructions for bypassing the phone tree for many different companies. That website is http://www.gethuman.com.

Save Money on Electricity

There are new technologies coming out each day that will allow people to save money on their electric bill. One such technology is available at hardware retailers. It is the programmable thermostat. A programmable thermostat can allow a house to be warmer during the summer and colder during the winter when there is nobody around to complain about the temperature. These thermostats can be programmed to bring the home back to optimum temperature just before the occupants arrive home from work or school.

A hot water heater does not need to be running when nobody is at home. This is another place where a timer can help significantly reduce power bills.

Another idea is to switch from incandescent light bulbs to fluorescent or LED bulbs. LED bulbs or light are not quite developed enough to provide general lighting, but they are good for situations wheredirectional lighting is needed.

Another way to save energy is to unplug electronic items not in use. Many electronic items which are not being currently used still consume electricity while they are plugged in.Items that consume electricity when plugged in are computers, computer monitors, televisions, printers, battery chargers, radios, many DVD players, and many more. Many of these items will lose their settings if left without power. Others will retain their settings. Items that will retain their settings when power is removed should be placed on a separate power strip that can be turned off when the items are not in use. The author leaves his computer on at all times due to its use as a telephone system as well as a monitoring device for security and home automation. However, the monitor is unplugged when not in use.

Home Safety Hack

Anybody who has had an elderly person with dementia or a small child prone to playing with stoves realize how dangerous this kind of thing can become. One way to prevent an accidental fire caused from an electric stove being misused is to simply turn off power to the stoves when it is not in use. This is done at the breaker box. The breaker for the stove is usually a double gang breaker.

Extend the Trial Period of Shareware

Many shareware programs stop working after the trial period is over. However, in many cases, it is possible to extend this trial period by downloading a program called RunAsDate. RunAsDate is available by visiting http://www.nirsoft.net/utils/run_a s_date.html. This site also provides instruction on how to use this program. It works for many but not all shareware programs.

Driveway Alarms

For those who live in rural areas where wireless driveway alarms do not work, there are a couple of options especially for those who are handy with a soldering iron. Passiveinfrared motion sensors can be modified to provide an alarm as long as they are sheltered from the elements and direct sunlight. Two pair telephone cable can be used to provide power from an adapter and carry the audio signal to the home. The chime or speaker part of the motion detector is unsoldered with one end of the cable being soldered in its place. At the end of the cable that is fed into the home, the chime or speaker part is then soldered to the same pair of wires. The other two wires are soldered to the battery terminals and the house end is soldered or otherwise connected to an adapter with the proper voltage and current capability.

The hacks listed in this chapter provide a common sense solution to some inconveniences. Use of just one of this chapter's hacks justifies the cost of this book.

Glossary - Sorting out the mumbo jumbo

Asterisk – a program available for Unix and Unix clones such as Linux that instructs a computer on how to perform the task of a phone system

PBX – Private Branch Exchange - A system that allows telephones to call one another

blue tooth – a technology that uses radio signals allow a device to communicate with another nearby device. Blue tooth is used for wireless mice, keyboard, and to connect wireless earphones to cellular phones. Blue tooth is different from WIFI.

burn – the act of writing information to a CD, DVD, Blue Ray or other similar optical disc client – A computer that initiates a connection to another computer to get information (web browsing), email, news, or other services that are carried or hosted by the other computer. The other computer is known as a server.

download – receive a file from another computer or device

DVR – digital video recorder – a device or program that records video from one or more sources such as television signals, cameras, the Internet, or other sources to an internal hard drive or to a disc such as CD, DVD, or Blue Ray

e-book – A file stored on a computer or other device that is a digital reproduction

guest operating system – the

operating system that is run inside of a virtual computer or virtual machine

hack – the process of delving into the inner workings of a program, network, or device in order to find out how it operates or to modify or extend its capabilities. The term has also been hijacked to mean the process of breaking into computers, writing malicious software or committing other computer crimes. It is also used to describe and event where one or all of the above that has been completed.

hacker – a person who delves into the inner workings of a program, network, or device in order to find out how it operates or to modify or extend its capabilities. It also has been **hijacked** to mean a person who breaks into computers, writes malicious software, or commits other computer crimes.

host operating system – the operating system that is installed on a computer which is started when the computer is turned on

hot spot – a device or facility that provides WIFI Internet connections for a small area. WIFI is commonly found in some restaurants, coffee shops, and many book stores.

Internet – A world wide network of computers that are connected by various means. The Internet allows such services as the World Wide Web, email, newsgroups, instant messaging, etc.

Internet Service Provider – ISP – The company or person who provides a connection to the Internet iPad – a name brand tablet computer made by Apple computer.

iPod – a name brand device made by Apple Computer that plays music and sometimes videos that have been downloaded from a computer. iPod is sometimes used interchangeably with generic devices that are correctly referred to as mp3 players

key logger – a program or device that records which keys have been pressed on a computer's keyboard.

malware – a set of instructions that cause a computer to do things that a user would not normally consent to such as sending spam, recording and sending information to criminals without user permission, illegally storing and sending copyrighted material, deleting important files, etc. Examples of malware include, viruses, worms, backdoors, fake antivirus programs, etc.

<u>midi</u> – Musical Instrument Digital Interface – a protocol that enables equipped musical instruments, computers, and other related devices to synchronize and communicate with each other

<u>mp3 player</u> – a device that plays music that has been downloaded from a computer. Sometimes used interchangeably with iPod

<u>Kindle</u> – A name brand e-book reading device

<u>Linux</u> – A free and open source operating system that is a clone of Unix

<u>open source</u> – software or computer programs that have the source code

available for users

operating system – a set of instructions that instructs a computer (or other device) on how to interact with users, devices, and programs. Examples include Windows XP, Linux, Mac OS, Windows 7, etc.

PDA – Personal Digital Assistant – any type of small, hand held computer used to organize information or assist in business or personal tasks

peer to peer – a description of a network between computers that are operated by home and business users with each peer having approximately equal functions. Peer to Peer networks are usually used to sharefiles such as digital music, video's, ebooks, etc.

podcast – an audio talk show that is

posted on-line as an audio file. The name implies that an iPod is needed to actually listen to the show, but that is not the case. Just about any device that is able to play common audio formats can play back the show

PVR – personal video recorder – a device or program that records video from one or more sources such as television signals, cameras, the Internet, or other sources to an internal hard drive or to a disc such as CD, DVD, or Blue Ray

rip – the act of extracting music or video from a CD, DVD, or Blu Ray disc and storing it on a computer.

server – a computer that provides printing, data, storage, email, or other services to other computers. Computers on which web pages are hosted are considered a servers.

Computers connecting to the server are known as clients.

social engineering – the tactic of conning people into revealing information, opening a file or program, or otherwise getting people to perform actions that they normally would not do

tablet computer – a self contained computer that contains a touch screen display in a single, compact enclosure

upload – sending a file to another computer or other device

VOIP - Voice Over Internet Protocol fancy way of saying "Internet phone" or voice over Internet

WIFI – a type of wireless connection or network that is used in homes, businesses or small plots of land in order to provide a connection to the Internet. Wireless routers in home usually use WIFI to provide connection to the Internet for computers so equipped

<u>Zune</u> – a mp3 player made by Microsoft

Useful Websites

Default Passwords

http://www.cirt.net
http://www.defaultpassword.com
http://www.routerpasswords.com

Free Software

http://www.download.com
offers freeware and shareware.
http://www.filehippo.com
offers freeware and shareware.
http://www.freshmeat.net
offers free programs.
http://www.openoffice.org
offers a free office suite.
http://www.sourceforge.net
offers free programs.

Search

http://www.altavista.com
is a general search engine.
http://www.anywho.com
is a people finding search engine.
http://www.ask.com
is a general search engine.
http://www.dogpile.com
is a general search engine.
http://www.google.com
is a general search engine.
http://www.webcrawler.com
is a general search engine.
http://www.whitepages.com
is a people finding search engine.
http://www.yahoo.com
is a general search engine.
http://www.yellowpages.com
is a company finding search engine.
http://www.zabasearch.com
is a people finding search engine.

Video and TV

http://abc.go.com/watch

http://cnettv.cnet.com
http://is.rediff.com
http://multiply.com
http://photobucket.com/recent/videos
http://video.aol.com
http://video.yahoo.com
http://vision.rambler.ru
http://www.4shared.com
http://www.allthingsscience.com
http://www.atom.com
http://www.babelgum.com
http://www.bing.com/videos/browse
http://www.blinkx.com
http://www.blogtv.com
http://www.boatson.tv
http://www.bofunk.com
http://www.break.com
http://www.cbs.com/video
http://www.channel101.com
http://www.cnn.com/video
http://www.coffeeshorts.co.uk
http://www.dailymotion.com

http://www.flickr.com
http://www.flurl.com
http://www.hulu.com
http://www.imeem.com
http://www.justin.tv
http://www.metacafe.com
http://www.nbc.com
http://www.netflix.com
http://www.streamick.com
http://www.tinypic.com
http://www.truveo.com
http://www.tu.tv
http://www.veoh.com
http://www.worldtvpc.com
http://www.wtfhumor.com
http://www.yourfilehost.com
http://www.youtube.com

Default Passwords
(For Popular Modems and Routers)

3Com

(none)	admin
Administrator	admin
adm	(none)
admin	comcomcom
admin	(none)
admin	admin
admin	password
admttd	admttd
debug	synnet
monitor	monitor
Root	(none)
tech	tech
User	Password

Actiontec

(none)	(none)
admin	(none)
admin	password

Apple

(none)	password
(n/a)	password
(n/a)	admin
root	admin

Asus

admin	admin
(n/a)	admin

Belkin

(n/a)	admin
(none)	(none)

Buffalo (Airstation)

root	(none)

Cisco

(none)	(none)
(none)	(Cisco)

Administrator	changeme
Administrator	admin
admin	default
cisco	cisco
root	attack
root	Cisco

Dell

admin	password
root	calvin

Dlink

(none)	(none)
(none)	admin
(none)	public
(none)	private
Admin	(none)
admin	(none)
admin	admin
admin	password
User	(none)
user	(none)
user	user

Linksys

(none)	(none)
(none)	admin
Administrator	admin
admin	(none)
admin	admin
comcast	1234
user	tivonpw

Netgear

(none)	1234
(none)	private
admin	password
admin	1234
admin	admin
comcast	1234
super	5777364
superman	21241036

Netopia

netopia	netopia

admin	(none)
(none)	(none)

SMC

(none)	smcadmin
admin	(none)
admin	admin
admin	barricade
admin	smcadmin
Administrator	smcadmin
cusadmin	highspeed
smc	smcadmin

U.S. Robotics

admin	admin
cablemodem	robotics
root	12345

Zyxel

(n/a)	(none)
(none)	1234

admin

admin

1234

admin

Useful Programs

Computer Problem Solvers

Avast Antivirus
http://www.avast.com

AVG Antivirus
http://www.avg.com

Malware Bytes Antimalware
http://www.malwarebytes.org

Ccleaner Registry and computer cleaner http://www.piriform.com

Clonezilla Hard drive cloning DVD
http://www.clonezilla.org

Combofix Antivirus and anti rootkit
http://www.combofix.org

Little Registry Cleaner

http://sourceforge.net/projects/littlecleaner

Microsoft Security Essentials Antivirus
http://www.microsoft.com/security_essentials

Quick Fix Fixes common Windows Problems
http://www.softpedia.com/progDownload/XP-Quick-Fix-Download-134770.html
For XP
http://download.cnet.com/7-Quick-Fix/3000-2094_4-75024066.html?part=dl-10055425&subj=dl&tag=button
For Vista Win 7

Trinty Rescue Kit computer repair CD
http://www.trinityhome.org

Internet

Thunderbird email client
http://www.mozillamessaging.com/thunderbird

Firefox web browser
http://www.getfirefox.com

Chromium
http://www.chromium.org

Pan Newsgroup reader
http://pan.rebelbase.com

Miro multimedia player and searcher
http://www.getmiro.com

Frostwire peer to peer file sharing
http://www.frostwire.com

Vuze bittorrent file sharing program
http://www.vuze.com

Logmein remote access
http://www.logmein.com

Show My PC remote access
http://www.showmypc.com

Team Viewer remote access
http://www.teamviewer.com

Ultra VNC remote access
http://www.uvnc.com

Wireshark network analyzer
http://www.wireshark.com

Skype Video and audio telephony
http://www.skype.com

Linphone video and audio V.O.I.P.
client http://www.linphone.com

Pidgin universal instant messaging
client
http://www.pidgin.im

Publishing

OpenOffice Microsoft compatible office suite
http://www.openoffice.org

Audacity audio editing
http://audacity.sourceforge.net

Blender virtual reality and graphics creator
http://www.blender.org

AVStoDVD DVD authoring and burning
http://sourceforge.net/projects/avstodvd

GIMP Graphics editing
http://www.gimp.org

GIF Construction Set Graphics editor and compressor
http://www.mindworkshop.com/gifcon.html

Windows Movie Maker
http://www.microsoft.com/windo
wsxp/using/moviemaker/default/
mspx

Windows Live Movie Maker
http://explore.live.com/windows-
live-movie-maker

DVDFlick DVD Authoring
http://www.dvdflick.net

DVDStyler DVD Authoring
http://www.dvdstyler.de

Kdenlive Linux professional video
editor
http://www.kdenlive.org

ffmpeg video file conversion
http://www.ffmpeg.org

Index

7-zip 140

authoring 145, 334-335, 373-374
authorization 119, 256
authorized 242, 246, 308, 309
automated 289
automation 346
avoid 128, 152-153, 296, 305, 312
avoided 290
avoiding 222, 316
Avast 16, 30, 369
AVG 16, 30, 369
AVStoDVD 373

B

backdoor 354
band(s) 3, 101, 126
bandwidth 133
bank 226, 228-229, 282, 291, 298-300
bargain 299
barcode(s) 306-307
battery 26, 47, 237-239, 272, 345, 348

C

D

E

E-bay 80, 265, 315, 340
e-book(s) 109, 115, 331, 351, 355
emulator(s) 146, 185-189, 192
erase(d) 201, 251

F

file sharing 129, 132-135, 242, 319, 372
ffmpeg 375
FreeBSD 205-207
FrostWire 130-132, 372

G

game console(s) 146, 186-187, 189, 192
ghost calls 328
GIF Construction Set 163, 374
GIMP 142, 161, 374
go to person 334

Gnutella 130
G.P.S. 234, 240, 274, 284-290
GSM 97, 238
graphics editing 374

H

hardware repair 3

I

iPad(s) 105, 317, 354
iPod(s) 317, 354-355, 357

J

Java 130-131
JavaScript 36
journal(s) 114
journalist(s) 341
junk 318, 340

K

Kdenlive 147-148, 375

P

password recovery 24-25, 27
password reset 24
peer to peer 129, 135, 139, 319, 356, 372
Phantom Alert 289

Q

Quick Fix 39-40, 371

R

rar archives 140
red light camera 288
recover passwords 26
Revo Uninstaller 39
rip off 319
RunAsDate 348

S

SIP 64, 70-71, 75, 86-87

V.O.I.P. client 373
V.O.I.P. device 67, 69
V.O.I.P. provider(s) 63, 73-74
V.O.I.P. service(s) 63, 65, 67, 70
V.O.I.P. software 73

W

WIFI 94, 212, 222, 350, 353, 358, 359
Wireshark 373

X

x86 197, 206
x86-64 190, 197, 206
Xbox 106
Xtensa 197

Y

Yahoo 325
You Tube 36, 147, 148

Z